STRESS MASTER

Richard Terry Lovelace, PhD, ACSW

John Wiley & Sons

New York • Chichester • Brisbane • Toronto • Singapore

To the memory of the late
Earl Nightingale
whom I consider to have been
my most valued teacher.

This book is also dedicated to the clients, family members,
colleagues and friends who shared so freely of their questions,
insights, and experiences.

And to Brian and Chris, with the unconditional love this book
encourages.

Copyright © 1990 by Richard Terry Lovelace, PhD, ACSW
Published by John Wiley & Sons, Inc.

All rights reserved. Published simultaneously in Canada.

This publication is designed to provide accurate and authoritative information in regard to the subject matter covered. It is sold with the understanding that the publisher is not engaged in rendering legal, medical, or other
professional service. If legal advice or other expert assistance is required,
the services of a competent professional person should be sought. *Adapted
from a Declaration of Principles jointly adopted by a Committee of the American Bar Association and a Committee of Publishers.*

Reproduction or translation of any part of this work beyond that permitted
by Section 107 or 108 of the 1976 United States Copyright Act without the
permission of the copyright owner is unlawful. Requests for permission or
further information should be addressed to the Permissions Department,
John Wiley & Sons, Inc.

Library of Congress Cataloging-in-Publication Data

Lovelace, Richard Terry, 1942–
    Stress master / Richard Terry Lovelace.
        p.   cm.
    Includes bibliographical references.
    ISBN 0-471-51725-9
    1. Stress management.   2. Stress (Psychology)   I. Title.
RA785.L68   1990
155.9′042—dc20   89-77146
                                                                              CIP

Printed in the United States of America

91 10 9 8 7 6 5 4 3 2

Preface

We need to move toward and into the twenty-first century with a much better understanding of stress, what causes it, and how to most effectively deal with it. Right now, most people's knowledge of stress is on a level with the understanding of physical disease hundreds of years ago. A new era of medicine began when early scientists announced that small pox and other widespread illnesses were not caused by curses, phases of the moon, or sins. People learned that "germs," which couldn't be seen, heard, or felt, were making them ill and that, while filth didn't cause disease, it certainly fed the germs that did.

A major purpose of this book is to show you that the reasons you've been giving yourself for your stress are not actually its causes. Traffic jams, your job, your spouse, your personal history, or where you live are not creating your stress any more than curses are making people sick. The source of your undesirable stress is like germs; you don't see, hear, or feel it. *What truly causes your hurtful stress is your inaccurate thinking.*

Before we go any further, let me say very clearly to you that I'm *not* saying, "It's all your fault you have stress—after all, your inaccurate thinking caused it." Your thinking does generate your stress, but you don't know you're doing it. Your thoughts creating your stress is a no-fault mistake: you're doing it without realizing it.

I'd like to be able to truthfully say I discovered all by myself this wonderful realization that inaccurate thinking makes the trouble in our lives. Actually, many bright and talented people have been pointing fingers at inaccurate thinking for thousands of years. Recently, other bright and talented people have called it "dealing with your erroneous zones," "cognitive therapy," "rational-emotive therapy," and "cognitive-behavioral therapy." Since I'm certainly not the first discoverer, I'll settle for doing my best to make the connection of stress and thinking far easier to understand and believe. My book is the first I know of that applies a strongly thought-focused or cognitive approach specifically to stress relief.

To make it easier for you to understand and believe that inaccurate thinking is generating your harmful stress, *I will be bringing together the major thoughts ("germs") that truly create stress.* I will name them, describe them, and tell you why they're inaccurate. Then I will explain a number of ways you can effectively deal with what actually generates your negative stress. (Stress is negative when it damages more than it helps. Exercise, if done safely, benefits you; it creates positive stress. *Negative stress may well be the greatest single threat to your relationships, success, happiness, physical and mental health, and your very life.*)

At least two other aspects of this book are different and helpful. I point out that *the stress that often hurts the most is stress you don't even know about.* I call it "hidden stress." With the material explained here as a tool, you can discover whether you have hidden stress. The second unique aspect is *"stress protection"—how you can protect yourself from future stress by avoiding it.*

While it's true that inaccurate thinking causes your stress, it's also true that much of what you think is ultimately decided by how you feel about yourself. *How well you like yourself on the surface surely matters, but your "secret self-esteem" matters far more.* Your secret self-esteem, how you feel about yourself without realizing it, decides the accuracy of your thinking more than anything else. I'll give you the opportunity to learn about your surface and secret self-esteem and, if warranted, what you need to change them.

This book sprang from material I wrote for my family, friends, clients, and myself, to deal effectively with our stress. The original version was used extensively by a number of people (not only clients) I knew well. Their feedback gave me a unique opportunity to discover what helped or didn't help, what needed less or more exploration, and what content was needed or could be omitted. In a real sense, most of this book has already been broken in for you. Enjoy and benefit from the results!

To gain the most you can from your reading, I recommend that you do the following:

1. Make notes about any information that is especially meaning-ful to you. Write summaries of what you've read or re-write a section in your own words.

2. Complete inventories or answers to questions as you come to them; don't wait until later. Reading sections that discuss other topics before you answer or postponing your replies could affect the directness of your answers and reduce the benefit.

3. Reread parts of this book. You'll get more with each review.

4. As much as possible, apply what you read to yourself. From my own experience, I know how easy it is to read something about human behavior and think, "That's just how (some other person) is." I'm not suggesting that you *not* apply what you learn to understanding others; just avoid limiting it to that. You deserve the attention too.

RICHARD TERRY LOVELACE

Winston-Salem, North Carolina

Acknowledgments

I appreciate the assistance of my wife Judy and my sons Chris and Brian. Getting this book into print has been a family endeavor. Judy, a registered nurse, served as a reader and a good listener. Chris helped prepare the original manuscript and patiently (for the most part) taught me how to use the computer and word processing program. Brian took many of the photographs I used to make drawings. Most of all, the family put up with my preoccupation and absences while I wrote.

Special thanks go to my friends and fellow therapists, Virginia Stafford, ACSW and Ron Davis, PhD, for their services as listeners and readers. Their personal support and professional insights have been important contributions.

My editor at John Wiley & Sons, Katherine Schowalter, deserves more of my gratitude than anyone else associated with this book. Katherine, I very much appreciate your help.

Ginny Simpson provided many valuable insights into the art of writing and her sound reasoning and encouragement were strong influences. Pam Altman assisted with word processing the manuscript. Her encouragement and helpfulness made it exceedingly clear to me that this was more than a job to her.

I'm indebted to my profession (social work) and the School of Social Work at the University of North Carolina at Chapel Hill.

The late Earl Nightingale and the late Lloyd Connant did more than any other people I know of, to promote the mass dissemination of personal development information. They had a significant influence on me through the many outstanding audio tapes and programs they and their company (Nightingale-Connant Corporation of Chicago) produced.

Dr. Albert Ellis, coauthor of *A New Guide to Rational Living,* is a pioneer and major innovator in the thought-focused (cognitive) approach to psychotherapy. He calls his brand of that approach rational-emotive therapy (RET). His considerable energy, wit, and candor have been a definite and valued influence on me.

Dr. David Burns, in his book *Feeling Good,* did an excellent job of refining and clarifying inaccurate thinking and some ways of dealing with it to relieve depression. I am grateful for his very useful work.

Dr. Aaron Beck is recognized as the founder of the brand of thought-focused psychotherapy known as cognitive therapy. It is difficult for me to imagine that anyone in our part of the world, who is taking a thought-focused approach to helping others, has not been positively influenced, directly or indirectly, by Dr. Beck.

Dr. Wayne Dyer, author of *Your Erroneous Zones* and so many other valuable books and audio tapes, has been inspirational.

I appreciate the help of the many thousands of people I've worked with over the years, in seminars and in individual treatment. Their questions, comments, challenges, and enthusiastic responses have been absolutely indispensable. I promise to do my utmost to pass along the help they gave me to as many others as I can.

The content that matters—the insights and truths—is real and comes from actual experiences of people I know or have known. Similarities between anyone described in this book and an actual person are entirely coincidental.

The drawings come from a variety of sources. Some were done from photographs my son Brian and I took. A few are adaptations of clip art I purchased and public domain art found in various books. Two of the drawings were inspired by Caldwell. The remainder came from my efforts to mimic sketches in some "how to draw" texts.

R.T.L.

Contents

1

You Can Get There from Here

*Identifying Your Stress and the
Benefits from Overcoming It*

"It's a record. I spent three days—no, three and a half days—with my mother, and we didn't argue. I didn't even yell at her once. Before, Mother would have driven me crazy (or I would've thought so) with her criticisms of me and with being so wrapped up in herself. There isn't any doubt about it. These concepts of yours really do work.

"And another thing: I went ahead and called two difficult clients this week. It turned out well. Unlike before, I stayed calm and handled their usual concerns much better. You don't need to pat me on the back for it, though. I've already patted myself." Sally flashed a broad smile. Seated facing me, confident and with her head held high, she seemed to have grown a couple of inches. Just two months before, this highly professional and oh-so-perfectionistic business-woman had come to counseling very upset. She was often irritable, had trouble sleeping, and had other symptoms of dangerous excess stress and depression.

Steven was referred to me because he (and his wife Gloria) suffered from the most common sexual disorder in men. He finished

"Watch out—I'm under a lot of stress!"

sex quickly, leaving Gloria far from satisfied. Actually, even though he finished, Steven wasn't satisfied either. Far from it.

During our second interview, I gave him a copy of some written material that later became part of this book. The material contained an inventory you'll find in Chapter 10. Gloria had wondered whether Steven had a drinking problem. The inventory was used to help him decide whether he had a problem with alcohol. He did.

A few weeks later, we'd nearly finished our work but hadn't talked again about the contents of the written material. During a session, Steven made a surprise comment. "By the way, my cholesterol is down." Then he credited the lowering of his cholesterol, the loss of five pounds, and the end of his drinking alcohol to his use of the information in the material I gave him.

"And I've got fingernails now," Steven said proudly. "I don't remember ever not biting my fingernails. And I wasn't even trying to stop biting them. It just happened." We talked about how his not biting his fingernails also signaled a significant lessening of his stress.

He'd recently noticed that he was sweating less. "Before I started using what's in your book, I used to get embarrassed because I was so wet. And it always happened when I was about to go into an important meeting. Now when I'm getting tense, I'm able to talk myself out of it." Clearly he did it quite well.

Steven's progress in becoming a stress master was particularly rewarding because at first he didn't realize he was stressed. If asked about being troubled, he would've said that he knew his job put "a lot of pressure" on him at times, and he was worried about the sexual problem and its effects on Gloria and his marriage. The reason for the premature ejaculation was pretty much beyond him. He would have written off the nailbiting as a "bad habit" left over from childhood. He didn't think he "drank that much." Besides, he hadn't come for counseling because of stress. Gloria had spoken to their minister about the worsening state of their marriage. The minister had then referred Steven to me for help with the sexual disorder.

Sally, the perfectionistic businesswoman, and Steven are now practicing what I've named "stress mastery." *Stress mastery is a truly different approach to taking charge of the biochemical reaction in our bodies called "stress."* Instead of the old "let's learn to relax" method of stress management, stress mastery goes to the actual source of damaging stress and unhappiness: our thoughts.

But I've been told it was factors such as traffic jams, noisy children, money problems, and too much work that caused stress. Here you're telling me it isn't what I've been told it was. Instead it's what I *think* that causes stress. I don't see how that can be. And even if it is my thinking, wouldn't it have to be thinking I don't realize I'm doing? That sounds pretty complicated.

What follows in this chapter and throughout the book is a dialogue. If you want, you can imagine you're the one talking with me and asking questions. Picture us sitting together in the place where you're reading now. We both are at ease, alert, and eager to learn and share.

Chances are, when you got your learner's permit you thought driving was complex. But taking it in manageable steps, you learned to drive and began to feel comfortable with it. By the time we finish our surprisingly easy steps together, you'll understand what I mean about thinking and stress and you'll know exactly what you can do. But first, let's take a look at some of the gains you can expect from becoming a stress master.

What's in It for Me?

All right, what can I get out of reading your book?

This book contains stress relief that goes straight to the source of the problem. By going to its roots, you can deal with excess stress far more effectively and lastingly. You can also learn about, and become very good at, controlling your moods. If you are fearful, angry, or sad and want to change, you can put yourself in a better mood and stay there.

Typical approaches to stress management are primarily, or even altogether, concerned with helping to deal with anxiety or fear. While anxiety is well worth our interest, it's far from the only emotion people experience and want to change. Stress mastery helps in relieving fear, anger, guilt, sadness, jealousy, and worry.

So I can find out more about why I have stress and moods I want to get out of. I can also learn what to do about them—what works better and lasts. What else?

There is a growing awareness among healthcare professionals of a powerful association between levels of stress and physical well-being. Chronic high stress can contribute to problems such as headaches, back pain, stomach problems, obesity, cancer, and heart conditions. Frequent stress, with anger, can foster high blood pressure and stroke. Stress associated with depression can cause physical fatigue and lower the body's resistance to illness.

Stress: A Major Health and Economic Problem

Using information he gleaned from a *Time* magazine article, Earl Nightingale reported that as many as two-thirds of office visits to family physicians are to remedy stress-related health problems. Such problems cost American industry between $50 billion and $75 billion—that's right, *billion*—each year. Stress is a major contributor, directly or indirectly, to six of the leading causes of death in the United States: coronary heart disease, cancer, lung disease, cirrhosis of the liver, accidental injury, and suicide.

People who have a problem with weight often report that what they're eating—and how much—is very much affected by their level of stress and their moods. Whatever the connection (I'm convinced there often is one), problems with weight will be helped by stress mastery.

Are there other physical benefits related to stress mastery?

Yes. By consistently reducing your level of stress and maintaining a more positive attitude, you'll be better able to eat right and to exercise regularly. This, in turn, will further reduce your stress. (Later chapters give an easy-to-follow approach to proper eating and drinking and recommend exercises that definitely help.) The more you can do to relieve and even eliminate hurtful stress, the better your physical well-being is apt to be.

Having better health and possibly living longer are real benefits. Are there more?

Absolutely. You'll improve your relationships at home, at work, and most places between. The more often you're calm and thinking well, the more your relationships benefit. Anger, jealousy, fearfulness, and depression negatively influence your relationships, because when you're feeling those emotions you are blocked from feeling *love* and *trust*. Those are, of course, two basics of happy and lasting relationships.

You're also blocked from understanding other people's point of view. Stress and feelings such as anger actually affect your brain in such a way that you become much more interested in hurting other people than in understanding them. An ability and willingness to understand and empathize with others is another essential to good and productive relationships.

What you're saying is that the more I can control, rather than be controlled by, my stress and moods, the more I'll like and be liked by others.

That's largely true, but there's more. You'll find it easier to work cooperatively with others and solve problems more effectively and speedily.

Are there any other benefits for me in reading this book?

Yes, there are several more. Anxieties such as fears of public speaking, elevators, flying, rejection, and failure definitely affect people at work and away from work. This text helps reduce and even eliminate such fears or phobias.

You can also learn how to better influence children to be happier, healthier, and more successful. Parents I work with tell me, "I think my children might be doing even better with stress mastery than I am. They're learning it by watching and listening to me."

Also, you can far more effectively avoid procrastination. You won't put off doing what needs to be done now.

Increasingly, *you'll find it easier to be optimistic about the future.* You'll come to expect good experiences to happen. If there are problems, you'll realize they are the exception rather than the rule in your life.

Can stress mastery do anything about burnout?

Definitely; it can help to avoid or cure burnout. There has been much talk and many pieces have been written about burnout—people finding their life at work or at home too much for them. Burnout occurs when individuals become increasingly overwhelmed with stress along with feelings of failure, frustration, hopelessness, and anger. Hurting so much, they begin to look for avenues of "escape." Some choose extramarital affairs or divorce. Worst of all, some choose fast or slow personal or career suicide. (Later on, I'll describe these reactions as "duck roasting.") Slow personal suicide includes behaviors such as excessive use of alcohol and cigarette smoking.

Burning out at Work

Still another benefit you'll discover is that you can concentrate better and think more clearly. Problem solving and studying will be easier. The reason is that excess stress and worry actually reduce (temporarily) your ability to use your intelligence. Stress gets you ready to run, fight, or hide rather than to think clearly. Worry slows you down and keeps you from focusing on the matter at hand. I see this frequently in my work with thousands of upset people facing a multitude of problems.

You'll find that others are less likely to influence you negatively. A spouse, or a sales clerk, will be unable to persuade you to accept or buy something you don't want. As you gain better control of your emotions, you'll be much less susceptible to hurtful influences.

Constructively asserting yourself will become easier. You'll think more of yourself because you will learn about and build your self-esteem. After reading this book, you're apt to like yourself better—permanently. If you're like many people who have heard this, you're probably thinking, "That's all right, but I don't particularly need self-esteem building."

"Burning Out at Work"

That's pretty much true of me, too.

What you'll readily learn here will positively affect how you feel about yourself at a deeper level. I call that feeling your *secret self-esteem*. It's extremely important; we'll cover it in detail in Chapter 4.

Finally, you can benefit by looking better. For example, people experiencing less stress and a better mood are more likely to smile. And a smile does more for your appearance than almost anything else in the world.

Is there something I can do to encourage myself to get the most out of this book?

It isn't at all required, but there is something. From the list below, pick out and write down the benefits that most attract you. *Keep your list handy and occasionally read it over to help keep yourself reading and learning.*

Read the Preface. You'll find some guidelines there for getting the most from this book.

Benefits of Stress Mastery

- ☐ Reduce damaging stress and keep it reduced.
- ☐ Get in and stay in a better mood. Deal much more effectively with sadness, worry, anger, jealousy, and guilt.
- ☐ Help prevent and gain relief from physical hurts such as headaches, back pain, stomachaches, and high blood pressure.
- ☐ Get weight under control—permanently.
- ☐ Improve relationships at home and at work.
- ☐ Deal effectively with life-interrupting anxieties such as fear of public speaking or fear of flying.
- ☐ Influence children to be happier, healthier, and far more successful.
- ☐ Overcome procrastination—stop putting off what needs to be done now.
- ☐ Feel more optimistic about the future.

☐ Avoid or cure burnout at work and at home.
☐ Find relief for career- and life-threatening addictions.
☐ Feel more like exercising and eating properly.
☐ Improve concentration and think more clearly.
☐ Avoid better the negative influences of others.
☐ Assert constructively, to get important needs met.
☐ Build self-esteem at all levels.
☐ Improve appearance and look better longer.

Taking an Inventory

To find out how much value this book can be to you, take the stress inventory on page 10. Study the headings on the scale of 1 through 7. After you read each statement, write the number on the scale below it that best says what's *usually true* of you. The larger the number you write, the more you believe the statement is true of you in recent times.

———————————

For a reason I'll explain later, it's important to take this inventory now.

———————————

Total the numbers you wrote down and then read the next paragraphs.

The highest possible score is 70. *The higher your score, the more you can obviously benefit from this book.*

If you scored 33 or less, you not only don't need this book, you may be able to write a better one. Another possibility, however, is that you were not being frank with yourself in responding to the statements. You may actually need this program's benefits more than most people do.

If you scored 34 to 39, you are in the lower range of people who have already completed this inventory. Chances are you're doing well, where stress is concerned. You already know a fair amount of what's here. If you read on and find that you don't, that means you were experiencing more stress than you realized. You have *hidden stress* that's a threat to you.

If you scored 40 to 46, you are in the middle range of those who've taken the inventory. You clearly need what's here.

Lovelace Stress Inventory

Not at All Like Me			Moderately Like Me			Just Like Me
1	2	3	4	5	6	7

1. I am under too much stress. [Remember, the *more* you believe a statement is *usually true* of you *in recent times,* the *larger* the number you write down elsewhere or circle below.]

1	2	3	4	5	6	7

2. I worry about people or things.

1	2	3	4	5	6	7

3. I have a fear that interferes with or holds me back in my life. [This may be a fear of situations such as speaking in public, driving long distances, being in deep water, or riding elevators.]

1	2	3	4	5	6	7

4. One or more of my relationships at work or at home suffers because of my irritability or anger.

1	2	3	4	5	6	7

5. I don't believe I'm as successful in my work as I can be.

1	2	3	4	5	6	7

6. The way I eat and drink is nutritionally very poor, or I eat too much fattening food too often.

1	2	3	4	5	6	7

7. I have a physical problem that I have been told or I suspect comes from pressures at work or at home. [Examples are: stomach troubles, sleep difficulty, teeth grinding, decreased sexual interest, high blood pressure, excess fat, muscle pains, excessive sweating, bitten fingernails, headaches.]

1	2	3	4	5	6	7

8. There are too many things I have to do each day.

1	2	3	4	5	6	7

9. I know or have been told I use too much of one of the following: nicotine from tobacco, caffeine from coffee or tea, alcohol, "nerve pills," marijuana, or hard drugs such as cocaine.

1	2	3	4	5	6	7

10. I exercise too little or the exercise I do doesn't help that much.

1	2	3	4	5	6	7

If you scored above 46, I've got terrific news for you. You have identified a wonderful opportunity. With this book, you can turn your life around. There is a great deal here that you don't know but very much need to know and apply.

Your stress inventory is a lot different from one I've seen before. That one had a long list of events people often experience, such as divorce and retirement, and gave them different numbers. Have you seen that one?

I've seen it and I've taken it three or four times over the years. That inventory has more than 40 life events identified as "stressors"— stress-causing happenings—and each one is given a number from 11 to 100. The greater the stress the event is supposed to create, the higher the number.

The last time I took that test was at a state social work conference. It was given free as part of an advertisement for a mental health treatment center. I scored a total of 354 because of events in my life, such as my sons' leaving home to begin college. My high score on the test told me I was experiencing a "major life crisis" and had an "80 percent chance of illness." I assumed the test meant *significant* illness, not something like the flu. The funny thing is that I've nearly stopped having even colds! I'm convinced that the reason for my improved health is my own stress mastery that comes from what I'm sharing with you in this book.

An acquaintance who has gone through a separation and divorce in the past two years scored just short of 900 on the same inventory. He certainly has had some tough times, but his level of stress is far lower and his mood is better than for a long period before the separation. He tells me that people who've known him for years comment on how calm he is and ask him how he's managing it. This gentleman has been using what this book recommends.

Are you saying that if things that happen in our lives, such as children leaving home to start college, or divorces, actually cause stress and then the stress makes us sick, you and some people you know wouldn't be getting healthier, happier, and more calm?

Yes, I am.

Where's It From?

Where did the information in this book come from?

From friends, family, myself (at one time), and unhappy client after
unhappy client, I've often heard the same words: "have to," "makes
me feel," "can't," "it's not fair," "I just know." If it weren't for those
people, and particularly my clients, I wouldn't have realized there's a
real and important association between using those words and being
in hurtful moods and experiencing too much stress. Later, I'll gladly
share that association with you and tell you exactly how you can use
it to your advantage.

So What's New?

**Will I learn something here that I wouldn't be likely to find
elsewhere?**

Most definitely. You'll learn to deal with the *cause* of your stress
rather than just the symptoms and influences. The usual approach to
stress management goes like this: A variety of events going on in the
individual's environment are causing negative stress: traffic, personal
conflict, criticism, noise, reports due at work, bills, sickness of a loved
one. Even apparently positive events not ordinarily associated with
stress, such as holidays, are contributing. Drugs like alcohol, caffeine,
and nicotine may be adding considerably to negative stress.

The individual responds to these stressors with *particular physical reactions* that are defined as *stress*. They include the release of
chemicals such as adrenalin (which is produced in the body and released into the blood), increased blood pressure and heart rate, tensing of muscles, and decreased blood flow to arms and legs.

The stress reactions that need relief find an outlet in the emotions—chiefly fear and anger. These feelings spark physical actions
necessary to reduce the stress reaction built up in the individual. To
our ancestors this typically meant running away from the stressor or
physically attacking it, which has been called "fight or flight."

Typical Stress Management Perspective

The typical approach holds that stressors—people or
circumstances that cause stress—bring about stress reactions

such as tensing of muscles, decreased blood flow to arms and legs, and higher blood pressure. These reactions result in emotions—primarily fear and anger. The emotions then spark activity intended to relieve the stress reaction by dealing with the stressor.

| Stressor | ⟶ Stress Reaction ⟶ Emotion ⟶ Activity |

Small to perhaps moderate amounts of stress reactions are all right and even helpful. They help us to get things done at home and at work. Without some stress, we might sit around and get little accomplished. Life would be less interesting.

Problems develop when the level of stress becomes and stays higher than necessary. Since running away and physically fighting are no longer acceptable releases, the stress level remains high and we're, in a sense, "stewing in our own juices." Serious physical problems can result, as can mental disorders such as depression, phobias, and panic attacks. Addictions to various drugs such as alcohol and nicotine may occur. In the long run, those addictions cause more stressors and therefore more stress. Work and family relationships suffer, in part, because of our tendency to mistakenly view others as threats to our safety. We "run away" from people and invest less in verbal and emotional expression, or we "attack" others verbally (not physically, I would hope).

So some stress probably helps, but a higher level can do serious damage to us and to others we come in contact with.

Yes, and an element important to understand is that, for many people, their level of stress is chronically too high and they don't realize it. They have "hidden stress," which may have built up so gradually over the years these people didn't notice it. The stress is so constant that they now think of it as being normal.

Living with hidden stress is similar to a cruel experiment. I've heard about this experiment from three different sources. Each time, a frog was used. For a reason that'll be evident later, I am taking "literary license" and substituting a duck for the frog. Please understand I'm *not* recommending the experiment. Researchers have taken a duck and put it in a large bowl with some cool water and

placed that bowl over a source of heat. Then they very gradually increased the heat so the water became warmer and warmer. In most cases, the duck stayed in the bowl to be boiled alive, even though it could easily have gotten out. If the side of the bowl was thumped, however, the duck jumped out before it was crippled or killed.

There are many people who are suffering greatly and don't recognize it. They have the common symptoms of chronically high stress, but they don't seem to recognize that their lives are all that unusual.

They are like the duck in the hot water—they don't know how much they are hurting because they're distracted and have gotten used to it. They are in danger of being "boiled alive" to the point of being crippled or even dead. Their mental health, careers, and relationships are at considerable risk.

Francine and Jake were telling me about the state of their marriage—a state just south of "the pits." Both of them had taken the Lovelace Stress Inventory. Francine's score said she was experiencing moderate stress. But Jake scored low, showing little stress at all. When he boldly announced it was true that he had very little stress, Francine looked at him wide-eyed and her mouth went slack.

I told him it was difficult to imagine that he was having so little stress. His frequent irritation with Francine and his daughters at least pointed to substantial stress. Still, he maintained that he was one calm and laid-back person.

When asked about physical symptoms of stress, he said he had none. His wife asked, "What about a couple of weeks ago, when you had the chest pain and couldn't get your breath? You thought you were having a heart attack. At the emergency room they said it was your nerves. And you often have trouble sleeping. You're up walking the floors."

Jake brushed these off as no indication of undue stress. He wasn't lying. He honestly didn't recognize the level of stress that threatened his marriage, his relationships with his daughters, and his life.

Identifying Hidden Stress

With a total score of 39 or less on the Lovelace Stress Inventory, chances are you have significant "hidden stress"—the stress that builds up so slowly over time that you don't even know it's there. You take it as being natural, but it isn't. There are three key items on the stress inventory you completed earlier that can tell you if you have this hidden (and particularly dangerous) stress. Did you give yourself more than a four on item 6, 7, or 9? (Not all—just one is enough.) If so, you have hidden stress. Item 7 describes some of the common physical symptoms of higher chronic stress. Items 6 and 9 relate to "remedies" people commonly use to try to cope with too-high stress. These remedies don't work.

I take it you agree with much of what you've been telling me about earlier thinking regarding stress. How do you disagree?

The usual approach says the best ways to relieve stress are to (1) reduce or get rid of the stressors in the environment or (2) relieve the stress reactions directly, with relaxation training. I most definitely disagree.

I'll give some concrete examples of what I'm talking about in the next chapter. Meanwhile, here are just a few of the differences:

- Most stress management puts little emphasis on the role of human thought. The truth is that *what we think* is of the greatest importance to the relief of stress, to happiness, to success, to good relationships, and to our mental and physical well-being. Stress mastery helps fill that essential link missing in typical stress management.

The Stress and Mood Mastery Perspective

What you think and how accurately you think determine the
amount of stress in your life and how well you manage stress.
By managing your thoughts, you determine the degree of stress
you experience and you control the emotions, thoughts, and
actions that result. Emotions such as anger, depression, and
fear come from stress. Usually these emotions are at least
inappropriate; they are attempts to deal with your built-up
stress. The conscious or subconscious thoughts and actions that
are sparked by the emotions are often equally inappropriate.
For instance, "I feel so bad [the conscious thought], I'll drink
beer [action] until I feel better." Alcohol doesn't solve trouble;
far too often, it makes trouble. The actions you take contribute
to increasing the influence that preceded your mistaken
subconscious thinking. In other words, you're in a cycle. The
more stress you have, the more you are likely to have.

You need to understand: *the thoughts that are causing your
stress happen so deeply or quickly that you don't even know
they're there. You have an illusion (false belief) that the thoughts
aren't present.* An "influence" (imagined or actual event such as
loud noise) seems to cause the stress reaction. It doesn't at all.

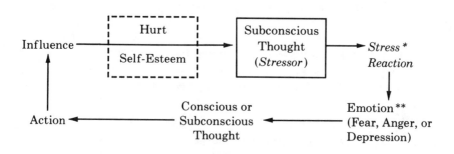

Influence —— [Hurt / Self-Esteem] ——→ Subconscious Thought (*Stressor*) ——→ *Stress* Reaction* ——→ Emotion** (Fear, Anger, or Depression) ——→ Conscious or Subconscious Thought ——→ Action ——→ Influence

---

*This is the negative stress that this book most effectively deals with. It isn't
normally the stress caused by bodily injury, exercise, or drugs.

**"Unpleasant" or "negative" emotions such as these aren't considered, by stress
masters, bad or good, right or wrong, desirable or undesirable. Most often they are
viewed as unnecessary means of relieving unnecessary stress. Experiencing such
emotions usually points to a lack of stress mastery skill in the person having them.

- Stress mastery *pays attention to the specific, inaccurate subconscious (unknown to you) thoughts or ways of thinking that are the actual cause of your stress.* Just as it is essential to discover which germ is causing a disease, it is often important to know what thought or way of thinking is causing your stress. So far, 27 thoughts or ways of thinking have been identified for you.

- Stress mastery focuses as much on your feelings, emotions, or moods as on the biochemical reaction to perceived threat (stress) that creates them. You *can* be happier and free from needless fear, anger, guilt, and sadness.

- Other programs give only superficial attention to exercise and food as they relate to stress relief and better moods. This program gives detailed and accurate attention to these essential areas.

- You're told about hidden stress, perhaps the worst kind of stress you can have. Your life, health, and relationships can depend on determining and dealing with your hidden stress.

- Stress mastery brings to light the one factor that ultimately decides how much stress you are likely to experience in your lifetime. That factor is your secret self-esteem.

- A largely unknown relationship between addictions and stress is revealed and explored. Often, without realizing it at all, people actively work to keep their stress, in order to avoid the awareness that they're addicted. "No wonder I [smoke, drink, overeat]. Look at all the stress I'm under."

From the list of benefits we went over earlier and the inventory I took, I have a good idea of what I can get. But I'd like to know something. Do you personally practice stress mastery?

I definitely use what I've created or considerably refined and offer you. I think of myself as staying out of my own hot water and at the same time thumping the "duck bowls" of others. Many people are in warm water that's getting hotter and more hurtful by the day. Others are already in life-threatening hot water and seem to barely know it.

No one lives forever, but your time and mine can be longer, more comfortable, happier, and more productive. Let's go for it!

2

Mark and Claire—Doing What Causes Stress

*Examples of the Thinking That
Creates Stress and Hurts Self-Esteem*

Mark sat in his small, poorly lit, and sparsely furnished office. He tried to work up enough nerve to call a prospective client. To himself, he reviewed notions that often came to his mind—in fact so often he hardly noticed what he was thinking. "What if he [the prospect] has already decided to buy from someone else? What if I say the wrong thing and lose the sale? I know my boss will fire me."

Mark's palms were moist, but his hands were cold. His stomach felt queasy and a nagging pain was growing between his shoulder blades. Aware that these were common symptoms of stress, he told himself, "This is silly. I shouldn't be so upset over a simple phone call. Nobody else has this much trouble."

Getting after himself didn't help. Mark decided to wait and maybe make the call later in the afternoon. He had some admittedly trivial paperwork he could do in the meantime, and he hadn't rearranged his desk in three whole days.

His busywork was interrupted when his supervisor stopped at his door. "Made that call to Sid Goldstein yet?" Mark said he hadn't and gave a feeble reason. He could tell his supervisor wasn't happy and was growing tired of his excuses. His job was in jeopardy.

By 5 P.M., Mark was definitely ready to unwind. He thought, "I've been under a lot of pressure all day. I deserve to cater to myself just a little." On his way home he made a quick swing by the convenience store. He found it convenient to buy a two-dollar bag of candy and several cans of beer. He was sure the cashier's look of disgust meant she was imagining him taking gulps of beer between handfuls of candy. Mark felt ashamed of his purchases.

But Mark had no intention of drinking beer with his sweets. He finished off the bag of goodies as he drove the remaining ten minutes to his home. As he turned into his driveway, he choked down the last mouthful and stuffed the empty bag under the seat of his car to join the other empty bags already there.

There were a couple of reasons why Mark secretly ate the candy. The first was the shame he felt over his weakness for candy. The second was that his children, ages five and seven, would expect him to share. The candy was his!

He didn't need to worry about the children drinking the beer. The hurt looks and comments of his wife were something else. She would ask, in a most disappointed way, "You going to drink all that beer again tonight?" Angrily, he would say something cute and meant to hurt: "No, I'm going to take a bath in it."

Mark would spend the rest of the evening angry or down in the dumps and would drink himself to sleep in front of the television. His

wife would tend to the children and go to bed early, to sulk. Mark hardly talked to his sons, much less helped take care of them. Only the relationship he had with his wife was worse than the one he had with his boys.

Despite his promises to himself that he would get his fat self up early the next day and jog a couple of miles, he woke up later than he had planned. He thought, "No need to get up and start exercising, since I'll have to stop early to make it to work on time." So, he turned over and went back to sleep.

Awakening late for work, Mark rushed to get to the job he increasingly hated. Chances were growing that he wouldn't need to hate the job too much longer. He would soon lose it, or the combination of stress, obesity, and alcohol abuse would kill or cripple him.

Another Example—Claire

Claire was referred to counseling by her supervisor. To him, she frequently seemed sad and on the verge of tears. She had headaches and too often left work early in the day because of them. She also related poorly with several of the women she worked with. The resulting hurt feelings and anger were disruptive to the entire department.

"They just don't like me," explained Claire. "They say mean things and hurt my feelings. I think the women are just jealous of how well I get along with the guys who work with us." When asked about the possibility that she was often stressed and sad, she seemed to deny she was. Then, as she continued to talk, she told of how she didn't like the way she looked. "I look in the mirror and say, 'You're ugly and fat.'"

During a later interview, she reported that when she was a child, her family moved frequently. Her father was an abusive alcoholic and her mother had "mental problems." They were poor, and often she went to bed hungry.

Some Common Characteristics

Both Mark and Claire were highly stressed and in "bad moods." His moods varied from fearful to angry, to guilty, to depressed. Hers were more consistent. She was regularly in a sad mood with brief episodes of anger mixed in.

If you were to ask Mark what accounted for his stress and hurtful moods, he would most likely tell you, "You'd be upset, too, if you worked for a supervisor like mine. He stays on my case all the time. My office is depressing and so noisy I can hardly hear myself think. Selling is hard work and high-pressured. People are all the time telling you 'No.' There's a lot of rejection in selling. A lot of it is luck—most of it bad, in my case. Besides all that, my wife and I aren't getting along. She's a nag—all the time complaining about one thing or another and treating me like a child."

Claire would, at first, tell you that she didn't know what was bothering her. She didn't believe she had much stress. (There was much of the hidden kind.) She just seemed to get "blue" at times for no apparent reason and cried easily. If you were to press her for an answer she would place the blame for her sadness and fears on others hurting her feelings or on her childhood. She would say, "You'd be hurting, too, if you grew up the way I did. Can you imagine what it was like to be a child raised by a mentally troubled mother and a drunken and sexually abusive father?"

What's the Problem?

I take it you're implying that these things Mark and Claire talk about aren't the real source of the bad stress and moods. If not, what is?

Let me start with some background. You could tell a stress management expert about Claire and Mark and ask him or her what their problems are. The answer you get would go something like this.

"Our ancestors survived because they had a superior ability to respond to threats to their lives quickly, with strong emotions like fear and anger. If, for example, a lion or rabid wolf attacked one of our ancestors, he either quickly got angry and defended himself or he got frightened and ran away. Either way, his emotions were released through fighting or escaping.

"The problem is, we've inherited this ability to respond to threatening events much as our ancestors did. Since life is far safer for us than it was for our ancestors, nearly all of the threats to us don't actually threaten our lives. Unfortunately, we begin to respond to these 'threats' (as when someone breaks into the line in front of us in the grocery store) as though they were life-threatening. Physically, things happen: our blood pressure rises, our heart rate increases, and our muscles tense up. We get physically ready either to beat the heck out of somebody or to run away. But hitting people or running away isn't appropriate or acceptable, so we don't—not usually, anyway.

"All this pent-up physical reaction and the associated feelings of fear or anger keep getting stored up inside us. They build and build and aren't released.

"Because of what he has inherited from his ancestors, Mark responds to pressures applied by his supervisor, the requirements of his job, and his wife's criticisms as though they were life-threatening. The pressure builds in him and, in addition to experiencing various physical problems, he stays frequently fearful, angry, and guilty. He tries to 'medicate' himself with foods he considers to be treats, such as candy, and with alcohol. His 'remedies' help in the short run, but ultimately make matters far worse.

"Much the same is going on with Claire, with some exceptions. Her chronic fear and anger held inside are being transformed into depression." (Many professionals agree that depression is largely fear or anger turned inward.)

"While Mark's threats involve the actions of other people on a day-to-day basis, Claire's perceived threats often involve her frequent reliving or recall of much earlier behaviors of other people. She keeps thinking—consciously or subconsciously—of times in the past when she was mistreated. Also, her childhood equipped her poorly for dealing with the problems of adult life."

A stress management expert might also note, "Because both Claire and Mark have been under severe, negative stress for so long, they have, in a sense, forgotten how to relax. By learning again to relax and to remain more relaxed in situations that caused stress before, the associated negative emotions—fear, anger, depression, and guilt—will be reduced or even go away. Also, the stress-related physical problems will be relieved. So, let's teach Mark and Claire how to relax.

"It may also be that some of the environmental factors that were threatening and were causing stress can be eliminated, or at least modified. For example, perhaps we can get Mark into a quieter, more cheerful office. Maybe we can arrange for Claire to move to another department where there are few women since she gets along much better with men."

Hold on. It seems to me it would be running away from the problem, if you moved Claire to another department. And if

you teach Mark and Claire to relax, I still don't understand how that's going to solve anything.

Remember, I said these are the kinds of recommendations that might typically be made. I didn't say I would recommend them unconditionally. Changing environments—like moving Claire to another department or Mark to a better office—and learning to relax have their place and can be of value. However, it's my strong conviction they're not apt to be so helpful on a lasting basis. And I'm sure you're right. They're more like avoiding the problem or covering the problem over instead of dealing with it.

Things Have Changed

Today, Mark is much happier, but not because of learning to relax or getting a better office. His supervisor is definitely pleased with his work and his job is far more secure. Even more important to Mark, he feels good. He is calm most of the time—free from much of the apprehension, anger, and worry that plagued him for years. Physically, too, he is doing a lot better. He has gotten rid of 37 pounds of ugly, life-threatening fat and he hasn't drunk alcohol in quite a while. His blood pressure and cholesterol are both down to far safer levels. Mark's relationships at home have also improved. He enjoys his children and they are happily getting to know him better. The strain with his wife isn't what it was, but they still need to make additional progress.

My working definition of happiness is the absence of needless fear, anger, sadness, jealousy, loneliness, boredom, and other such feelings. Happiness is the natural emotional state of human beings.

Mark puts it better than I could when he says, "If anyone had told me just a few months ago I could be this much in control of how I feel, I wouldn't have believed it. I actually am happy most of the time. I enjoy my work and am doing a good job. The things I needed to do but hated before, I look forward to now. It's amazing! Overall, my life is a lot better than it was." He's well on his way to being a stress master.

Claire hasn't made the progress Mark has. She clearly likes herself better, and isn't so hard on herself as before. She's still in the same department at work but likes the women she works with better, and her headaches are less frequent.

The True Problem

The actual problem had far more to do with what Mark and Claire thought and how they approached living (they lived backward) than with the situations they were in or their childhood experiences.

A reason Claire had more difficulty than Mark in making progress was that she had more trouble believing what I told her. For example, I said to her, as I did to Mark, that whenever she was stressed and so, sad or angry it was because she was telling herself something that simply wasn't true. I told her that, as she increasingly told herself the truth and approached living differently, she would have much less dangerous and painful stress and fewer "bad" moods.

"I'm not a liar." Claire explained that she thought I was calling her a liar when I told her she was telling herself statements that weren't true. I responded, "Claire, I don't believe you're telling yourself untruths on purpose. I'm convinced you do tell yourself things that aren't true, but you do it without knowing it. You experienced many things growing up, and you explained the meaning of those experiences to yourself as best you could, as a child. Considering you did a lot of this interpreting when you were a child and didn't know nearly as much as you know now, it's little wonder you sometimes got the meanings incorrect. Those explanations of events from early in your life have stayed with you. All of them have been stored in your subconscious mind. Because they're subconscious, you don't even know they are there, but they affect your feelings and behavior every day.

"Let me give you an example. You were often mistreated as a child, right?" Claire agreed that she was. "Although you didn't know it at the time, you explained the abuse to yourself as punishment. You reasoned in your child's mind that to be 'punished' so severely and so often, you must have been a very bad person and 'stupid, too.' You were so 'stupid' that you didn't even know what you had done wrong. As a child, you identified yourself as a bad and stupid person and it has subconsciously stuck. You often, without knowing it, tell yourself that you are worthless and dumb. No wonder you're stressed and depressed."

These were only some of the insights I shared with Claire. Still, she had real trouble putting her new stress-relieving and happiness-promoting information into practice—even though ways of putting it into practice were clearly outlined for her.

You might sometimes, like Claire, get the notion that I'm implying something is wrong with you. Just keep on reading; you'll understand I'm not.

Misinterpretations as Children Lead to Misinterpretations as Adults

Some of the most hurtful misinterpretations that we make as children and that cause stress later have to do with love and acceptance. If we were seriously ill as children or as adolescents, we may have misinterpreted the concern people showed for us as being love. Of course, it wasn't love, it was simply concern. The concern may have come out of love, but it wasn't love itself. Later, when we are adults and become sick, we feel unloved when our spouse or others aren't concerned or become decreasingly concerned over our various physical complaints. "If you really loved me, you would be more attentive when I have such a terrible headache (or whatever)."

There are many other possible misinterpretations of love. An adolescent boy may hear, "A good girl won't do it [have sex] with you unless she loves you." Because of that misinterpretation, he later misunderstands his wife's lack of interest in sex as a loss or absence of love for him. That scares him, so he expresses his fear with a mean face (anger). He may sulk or get angry over substitute things, such as her not having dinner ready on time.

Three Principles of Human Experience

As time passed, Claire's well-deserved progress was clearly blocked by more than simply having trouble believing what I told her. Three principles of human experience were involved:

1. We tend to keep what we are used to.
2. We need attention from others.
3. Even problems and stress serve a purpose for us.

I need more explanation from you to understand these.

The first principle is that human beings try, without knowing it, to maintain what they are used to, even when what they are used to is hurtful. Most of us have heard true accounts of how people have spent years in prison and have paid their debt to society. But when they got out of prison they immediately did something that put them back in jail. As unpleasant as prison was, they were used to it.

Claire was used to being stressed and depressed. Without being aware of it, she sought to keep what she was used to.

The second principle of human experience that interfered with Claire's progress was that human beings crave attention from others and will get the kind of attention they are accustomed to in ways that they are most familiar with.

Claire was accustomed to negative attention—people paid attention to her because they were upset with her or "bothered by" her behavior. Claire was unwittingly seeking negative attention. Being sad and angry was an attention-getter for her, although she didn't know it and would not have admitted it if she did. Unknown to her,

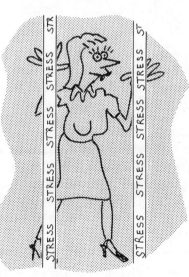

Claire wasn't sure she could get the attention she craved if she were calm and happy; and, as strange as it might seem, she actually feared being calm and happy because she wasn't familiar with that condition. Human beings so often fear the unfamiliar.

The third and biggest obstacle to Claire's acceptance of the truth was that emotional pain and stress served a "useful purpose" she was entirely unaware of. The pain served to punish her for the "bad things" she imagined she had done in the past. Without realizing it, she "beat herself up" with her stress and sad mood.

So it isn't because we're bad that we sometimes keep from making progress in dealing with problems like too much stress. Even our resistance is intended to accomplish something worthwhile.

I want to share with you what Mark has made good use of and Claire will, I'm convinced, someday make even better use of.

In the chapters that follow, I'll tell you exactly why you, I, and everyone else experience needless stress, fear, sadness, guilt, worry, and anger. What's more, I will tell you what you can do, and I mean CAN DO, to be free of those hindrances to a happier, longer, and far more successful life.

Let me note here that I've been interested in "how to be happier" or "how to deal with excess stress," or whatever you want to call it, for myself and my clients for many years. To satisfy that interest, I've read a number of books. While I usually believed that the authors were offering their best and sincerely wanted to help, their recommendations on what to do to be rid of excess stress or to be happier seemed impossible. It was as though they were saying, "To be happy, first you put a finger through a ring that fits snugly and then you grasp that finger and with one mighty jerk, you pull the rest of your body through the ring." Not at all likely!

Finally, I'll share how you can best gauge your progress. By doing that, you'll be far more likely to maintain what you've gained.

Let's move along to more specifics.

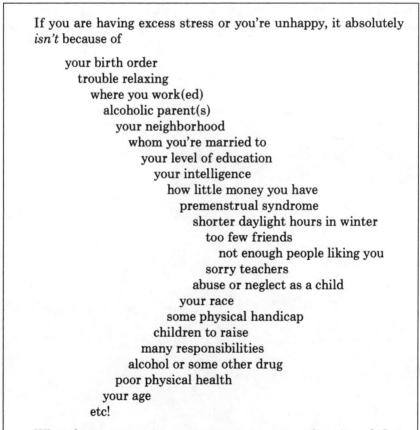

If you are having excess stress or you're unhappy, it absolutely *isn't* because of

> your birth order
> trouble relaxing
> where you work(ed)
> alcoholic parent(s)
> your neighborhood
> whom you're married to
> your level of education
> your intelligence
> how little money you have
> premenstrual syndrome
> shorter daylight hours in winter
> too few friends
> not enough people liking you
> sorry teachers
> abuse or neglect as a child
> your race
> some physical handicap
> children to raise
> many responsibilities
> alcohol or some other drug
> poor physical health
> your age
> etc!

What does account for your excess stress or unhappiness? One thing: *your incorrect and subconscious thinking,* coming from mis-interpretations of one (or probably more) of the above.

Does this mean we shouldn't do what we can to get rid of drugs, clean up neighborhoods, fight poverty, improve medical care, and education?

Far from it. I have many colleagues who are reaching out and even risking their lives to help make such improvements. I have only respect and support for them and their efforts.

I compare the situation to the relationship among germs, filth, and disease. Some germs (some thinking) cause disease (stress and unhappiness), and filth (drugs, poor neighborhood, abuse as a child, lack of education, too little money, and so on) feeds germs. The program I'm offering can be compared to a laser light that zaps the germs, no matter how much filth there is. My program goes to the cause. There's still more than enough justification to clean up the filth as best we can. But we don't need to wait for the cleaning to be done to be safe.

3

Living Life Forward

*The Approach to Life That Discourages
Stress and Helps Self-Esteem*

"I don't understand why I feel so bad. Look at what I have—a new sports car, a really good job, an expensive house, and lots of friends. I should be on top of the world."

But Don wasn't on top of the world or of anything else. He was approaching middle age and burning out on his career, which seemed less and less important to him. During most of the time he spent at home, he was angry or eager to find some excuse to go out with his friends and have a good time.

His anger at home was most often directed toward his nearly grown daughter, whom he described as having no real interest other than "partying" and "talking for hours on the phone."

Coming from a family where no one owned or had accomplished much and no one was all that happy, Don decided (and didn't know it) early in life that the secret to contentment was to get a good education, find a high-income job, and amass the "finer things in life."

Another Example

A young woman I'll call Wanda said, "I can't take my tranquilizer anymore. I can't work. I can't sleep. I can't lose weight. I know I should but I just can't stop worrying." Those were just five of a dozen or so of her statements using the word "can't" in about twenty minutes of talking with me.

Her physician had become concerned that Wanda was addicted to tranquilizers and referred her for an evaluation. She visited the physician regularly with various complaints. Chief among them were chronic muscle and stomach pains caused by high levels of obvious and hidden stress.

"I just know I'm going to get cancer." Wanda explained that many relatives on her mother's side of the family had gotten cancer and died from it.

Wanda readily described herself as a "worrier." She worried about her husband, her parents, her brothers and sisters, her friends and neighbors. When asked how she became such a worrier, she said she guessed she "got it" from her father, who had always worried a lot too. "But if you love someone, you worry about them," she added. "Also, I worry about people because if I don't, something bad might happen to them."

Wanda experienced considerable guilt, but usually wasn't aware of how guilty she felt. She was a deeply religious person and grew up in a "wonderful family." Wanda felt guilty about how often she got angry at her husband, who was loving, and slow to get upset. She felt guilty about not wanting to have more children; her husband wanted them so much. She had this same sense of blame for much of what happened to others. She felt varying amounts of guilt when something "bad" happened to family members and others she knew. Somehow Wanda sensed she had caused those "bad things" to happen.

Although they had very different backgrounds, interests, and concerns, Don and Wanda were alike in several ways. They both felt stressed and unhappy too often and both wanted to feel better more of the time. Both were sensitive people who honestly cared about others. They were articulate and bright, although both of them would have expressed doubt about how intelligent they were.

Living Life Backward

Wanda and Don had something else in common, something they shared with all people who are hurting from stress and are unhappy; all people who are not yet stress masters; all people who are more angry, sad, fearful, jealous, or tense than they want to be. Both Wanda and Don, in an extremely important way, lived life backward.

What do you mean by that?

People who are unhappy because of excess and damaging stress think that they need to

- Do something in order to
- Have or get something that will make them
- Be someone who is of value or worth.

The key steps for them are:

$$Do \longrightarrow Have \longrightarrow \boxed{Be}$$

Don believed, "By getting a good education and a better job [the Do part] I'll Have a lot of money, expensive cars, and many friends, and I'll Be happy, of greater value, and worthwhile." Don was sure he would then like himself better.

Wanda believed that by worrying—thinking about negative events that had happened or might happen that she could do little or nothing about—or by taking the blame for negative happenings she wasn't responsible for (the Do part), she would then Have the attention of others—and the sense that she controlled the feelings and lives of others. Because she got the attention of others and controlled them, she thought, without realizing it, that she would Be happy, satisfied, of value, worthwhile, or important. She would like herself.

Because their approaches to life were, in fact, backward, Don and Wanda didn't make it to the Be part of the process. They didn't have a deep-down, genuine, and lasting liking of themselves. They didn't think they were worthwhile.

Hold on. Are you telling me that I may be like Don and Wanda—that I may have a messed-up, backward approach to life?

What I want to get across is this: you may not be in charge of your level of stress and its effect on your happiness. To whatever degree you are dissatisfied with your life and feel unsuccessful at home or at work, you have been unwittingly taking an approach that will not work for you or anyone else. As long as you take the "Do to Have to Be" approach to life you'll not be fully satisfied or live as happy, complete, and productive a life as you're capable of living. More to the point, and what we're here to talk about, you won't be free of the stress you have (and may have even more than you know) that's threatening your life, health, relationships, and career.

You'll be tempted to apply what you learn to other people: "You know, that's just life . . . ." To get the most you can from this book, it's essential that you apply what you learn to *yourself*. Seeing the ideas here only as they relate to others can be a subconscious strategy to avoid making the changes *you* need to make.

I didn't intend to encourage any such notion that I thought you had messed up or you were somehow bad for taking this approach. I take the stance that if you're doing what doesn't work and won't work, it isn't because you knowingly want to be less happy than you're capable of being. It's because you don't yet know and practice a successful alternative.

Living Life the Way It Works

What's this alternative that does work?

The approach looks like this:

$$\boxed{\text{Be}} \longrightarrow \text{Do} \longrightarrow \text{Have}$$

You start with the Be part—with being someone. Because you are someone of real value—worthwhile, deserving of love, and loved no matter what—and because you Be someone already, you then Do something and Have what you desire and truly deserve.

I'm not sure I understand what you're saying.

Remember how Don started out believing that his value, his right to or "deservingness" of love, depended on such things as making money, getting career advancements, and having friends? Don believed that once he had done these (the Do part) he would then Have companionship, new cars, a wonderful house, and prestige in his job. And because of all this he would then Be loved, successful, worthwhile, and satisfied.

I first saw Don because, nearly halfway through his life, he had finally realized that to Do and to Have had not made him content or comfortable. He felt anything but loved, worthwhile, and satisfied.

Unconditional Love

Are you saying I shouldn't want to make a good deal of money and have nice things like a new car and an expensive home? It seems to me that if I'm not trying to better myself, I'll just be complacent and unsuccessful.

Attempting to Do and to Have so that you can "better yourself" (think better of yourself and have others think better of you) uses *fear* as your motivator. "If I don't get this job [or, if I don't worry about others, if I don't get married, and so on] I won't Be a better person, a happy person, a loved person."

Basing what you Do and Have on what you Be means using *love* as your motivator. You Do and Have because you absolutely deserve "the good life." When you switch over to using love as your incentive, instead of fear, it's like switching over to the best, cleanest, highest-octane gas you can buy, after trying to run your car on watered-down gasoline. Your car runs beautifully; your life takes off!

But I do use love as my motivator. I love my family and I work hard for them because of it. I love my country and my friends, and so I do a lot for them.

The kind of love I'm talking about is something different. It means loving yourself as much as you love others. And it means loving others and yourself no matter what—*unconditionally.*

Remember I said earlier that Don wasn't getting along with his daughter?

Yes, I remember.

According to Don, she was only interested in partying and talking on the phone. He wanted her to go back to school, get a good education, and have a worthwhile job. Only when she showed some inclination to do what he wanted was he consistently affectionate toward her. His love was conditional: for him to love her, she was required to Do (go to school) and Have (a good job and education). His daughter saw their relationship as being manipulative. Love was held out as a "carrot" to get her to do "the right thing." So, she resisted his attempts to control her.

Chances are Don's daughter realized years before that her father's cars, fine home, and good job didn't make him calm or happy. So why should she bother to "get ahead?" Don seemed at ease and reasonably content only when he was talking with his friends and going out. She decided to do the same.

When we have conditional love for another person, that love will:

- Come across to the other person as a threat, which makes the love frightening. "I'm not going to love you unless you. . . ."
- Give the other person the impression of being manipulated or controlled. "Do what I want and I'll love you." The other person is likely to rebel against love on those terms.

■ Give a subtle message that we value the person only for what he or she can do or have, and that we think actions and possessions are more important than the person.

If we approach living backward ("Do to Have to Be"), we are conditionally loving and accepting ourselves also. For example, "I will like (love) me when I lose 25 pounds." This approach has the same negative influence on us that our conditional love has on others. We are more likely to think thoughts that make us feel threatened, manipulated, and of little value and to feel that only our actions and possessions are worth anything. No wonder we experience so much stress and aren't as successful as we might be!

Okay, I think I have the idea now. I need to start by accepting myself—caring about and loving myself unconditionally— and then base what I do and have in life on that. When I care about myself, I'll see to it that I succeed at work and home, I'll make a good income, and I'll make sure that I'm in charge of how I feel—my stress and moods.

Is It Selfish?

There are still a couple of things I wonder about. One is all this about caring about myself, and self-acceptance. Doing what I do and having what I have, based on this, seems awfully *selfish* to me.

The opposite of love isn't hate. It is fear!

When you are more self-accepting and self-loving you'll be more likely to love and accept others. Nothing is less selfish than increasing your capacity for loving others.

Besides, if anything were to be called "selfish," then being stressed and unhappy would definitely be selfish. Under stress, we get all wrapped up in ourselves and have "pity parties." It's far easier to give to others—to be loving of others—when you're calm, confident, and successful.

You needn't be concerned about being or becoming selfish.

True Self-Esteem

What was the other matter you were wondering about?

This talk about the need for self-love and self-acceptance gives me the impression you think I hate myself or at least don't like myself. I like myself pretty well. I think I like myself as well as most people like themselves.

An elderly physician I shared office space with years ago once told me, "There are two kinds of nervous tension: the kind you know about and the kind you don't know about. And it's usually the kind you have but don't know about that does the most damage." I didn't realize it at the time, but what he was talking about was similar to what I later identified as hidden stress.

Over the years, I've come to realize there are also two forms of self-dislike and even self-hatred; one you know about and the other you don't. The kind you usually don't know about does, by far, the most harm. Subconsciously you may feel dislike and even hatred for yourself, but you simply don't know that those feelings are there. I call this "hurt secret self-esteem."

A somewhat extreme example of hurt secret self-esteem is a person who often says things like, "I'm the greatest! I am the very best!" Most professionals who've studied self-esteem will quickly tell you that such a person really has self-dislike—poor self-concept—but may not know it. People who use strong statements of self-liking are attempting to hide from others and themselves how badly they actually feel about themselves.

Criticism—making fun of or disapproving of others—is, in fact, an expression of the fear that one is wrong in his or her own beliefs, actions, or feelings. It reflects hurt secret self-esteem.

By bringing others "down," the criticizers think they'll bring themselves "up."

I thought such people were egotistical and felt too good about themselves. Has the opposite been true all along?

That's right. People who repeatedly make a point of telling you how well they think of themselves are in fact saying to you, "I don't like me." People who have genuine self-love will rarely, if ever, brag or talk about how well they feel about themselves. They assume their value is obvious to others, with no need to talk about it.

What Is and Isn't Me

Does self-love or self-acceptance mean you like everything about yourself and you don't want to change anything? Does it mean feeling self-satisfied or complacent about yourself?

Yes and no. Self-love that's unconditional (the way it very much needs to be) means you like everything about yourself. You don't want to change anything that's truly you. At the same time, you realize you are much more than what you do and feel. You may well want (and work) to change what you do, think, or feel. What's truly you is what was you at the time of your first breath. Everything else has been added since then and is not you.

I know, this is pretty deep stuff.

I believe I understand what you mean, though. What's uniquely me—what I came into this world with—is the real me that needs and deserves my unconditional love and acceptance. It's all right to want to change some of the things I've added.

Exactly. Experts who study young children say that early in life the children have trouble telling where they stop and others begin. Children identify so much with their mother that they think of themselves as being extensions of her. Usually around age two the children realize

they are separate people and not part of their mother. Their frequent use of the words "no" and "I won't" are a part of (and contribute to) their independence, their growth as individuals.

We confuse ourselves with our actions and feelings in much the same way that, as children, we have difficulty separating from our mother. Because we don't yet know any better, we take the position that, "I am what I do. I am what I feel. So, if I do [and think] and feel 'bad things,' then I must be a 'bad person.'" An essential part of human growth and maturity is to gain independence of that childhood perception.

We need to understand that we have been mistakenly throwing the "baby" (what we truly are) out with the "bath water" (behaviors, thoughts, and feelings we found unacceptable). Getting "fresh water" is great, but have mercy on the innocent "baby."

So one characteristic of people who "Do to Have to Be" (backward living) is that they confuse their behavior and feelings with themselves. Without realizing it, they conclude that if they are feeling and doing "bad," then they are "bad." But they really aren't. Are there other characteristics of people who live this way?

Yes, *procrastination*—putting off doing what needs to be done and usually putting off what *most* needs to be done. Mark, who was described in Chapter 2, put off calling his potential clients and placed his job at risk.

Those who "Do to Have to Be" are more inclined to (but don't always) procrastinate. And because of that procrastination they're more likely to suffer at work, in relationships, and elsewhere. They think that if they fail at a task—fail to Do or to Have—then they are failures. Horse hockey!

As we take the "Be to Do to Have" point of view, we realize that our performance says nothing about our value. In fact, so-called "failure" would only enhance our value. Each time something doesn't work out, we learn something; we know more than we did before and that knowledge increases our considerable worth.

I like this story about Thomas Edison. He had tried and failed several thousand times before he finally perfected the electric light bulb. During an interview, a newspaper reporter asked Edison, "How does it feel having failed more than 1,000 times before succeeding by making the first electric light bulb?" Edison looked at the reporter and smiled. "Son," he said, "I know more than 1,000 ways not to make an electric light bulb and one way to make one. What do you know?"

The point is that when we unconditionally love and accept ourselves (what's truly us) we do what we do and have what we have because we *are* worthwhile, not because we're trying to get to be worthwhile. We view each happening ("failure") that *doesn't* bring the final reward as a step in that direction. It's a learning experience that, if anything, enhances our value still further.

Do you mean I should get out there and do any old thing— it doesn't matter much what it is—and if it succeeds, it succeeds and if it fails, it fails? I shouldn't care one way or the other?

Because you know you're worthwhile, you are more likely to choose undertakings that are also worthwhile. And anything you undertake you're apt to do well. You'll care about what the results are, but even if they fall short, you will want to learn all you can and enjoy that new learning. A good learning experience is worthy of your enjoyment.

Because I am worthwhile, I do what's worthwhile. No matter the outcome; I learn and enjoy.

Wanting to Do Things Perfectly

Another characteristic of those who "Do to Have to Be" is *perfection-ism*. They are or tend to be perfectionistic—trying to behave per-fectly or as close to perfect as possible.

Brad was handsome, bright, in his early 20's, and doing nothing in particular. In his teens he had been an excellent golfer, but he gave up golf because his level of play didn't meet his standard, which was perfection. He dropped out of college for much the same reason. He didn't go to work because, according to him, there wasn't anything out there that was enough of a "challenge."

Brad said, "I'm sorry; if I can't do something extremely well, then I just won't do it very long." Fear of failing was the reason he gave for his attitude and it was getting worse almost by the day. His emotional reactions were depression and irritability.

When I asked him to rate his usual level of self-esteem on a one-to-seven scale, with seven being the best possible, he said, "I'm usually around a two, I guess." He had a pretty poor opinion of him-self. He knew he wasn't perfect, worthwhile, okay, worthy of love, or whatever you want to call it, because he didn't act perfectly or close enough to perfection.

Perfectionists lead their lives as though each activity were being graded by God. And they think that God gives only A's and F's. Every-one else is graded by the usual grading system: A, B, C, and even D are passing grades, and only F is failing. That gives perfection-seekers a considerable handicap. They have less of a chance to pass (succeed) than others who have a more liberal grading system. In their eyes, they do a lot of failing and their opinion of themselves suffers greatly.

I recall a true story I heard about two college professors. Both of them knew that their jobs depended, in part, on how often they wrote papers that were published in journals. One of the professors was a perfectionist and would send off one of his manuscripts only if he determined it was worthy of a grade of A. After some years of doing this, he realized that the other professor was advancing faster than he was. So the perfectionist professor said to his colleague, "I've seen the papers you've had published. They were all right, but not nearly as well done as mine. How is it that you are getting so much more recog-nition than I am? You're asked to give more talks, and it's obvious to me that the chairman of the department likes you better."

The other professor responded, "I'm sure the reason is that I get more papers published than you do. You're so picky, it takes you much longer to write a paper. I'm willing to send in a paper I wrote that's good, but far from perfect. If one journal turns it down, I'm not bothered. I just mail it to another. So, I get twice as many published."

When we take the workable point of view and start with unconditional self-love and acceptance, doing things perfectly is less important. We realize that, in the only way that truly matters, *we are perfect,* so behaving "perfectly" will neither raise nor lower our value and will not be more perfect than perfect.

Wait a minute. What do you mean, "we are perfect"?

What's truly us is what first came into this world. What we want to change (imperfections) are things added later. They aren't really us. There isn't now, never has been, and never will be another person in this world who is exactly like us. We are the only exact (perfect) example of us. And that's the only way any human can be perfect! Any other way of being perfect is a lost cause from the start.

But What about My Nose?

I agree most of that makes good sense, but I came into this world with a big nose. And my nose keeps me from being perfect. I also have this really terrible scar, and that makes me even less perfect.

When I say, "What is truly you is perfect," I'm not saying that you, and other people, like everything about your physical appearance. Still, your appearance is a part of what is exactly or perfectly you; there's never going to be another just like you. Each scar and irregular facial feature just adds to your uniqueness and your perfection as an individual.

As we increasingly take the "Be and Do and Have" perspective we find that features of our physical appearance that troubled us before bother us less and less until they no longer bother us at all.

Before you ask me: yes, you *will* take pride in your appearance. Just because you aren't bothered by what you once thought were physical flaws doesn't mean you'll let yourself go. In fact, you are likely to look even better. Self-confidence, happiness, improved physical well-being, and success in many areas can only further enhance your looks.

Far too often, I see people with "mean looks" on their faces. When I imagine them without those mean looks I realize they are easily what our society defines as beautiful or handsome. But they unwittingly hide it behind their stress and unhappiness. Others hide their beauty behind their obesity (excess body fat).

It Isn't So Easy

I can see some of the advantages to changing over to this new way of living. I just can't find the switch I'm supposed to flip to be calm, more successful, and in a good mood all the time.

Changing over to doing and having on the basis of no-matter-what love and self-acceptance isn't as quick as flipping a switch. It's a lifelong pursuit and *the only pursuit in life entirely worth the effort.* It is joyful, entertaining, invariably interesting, and completely satisfying—at least, it has been for me so far.

I've heard many people say they were afraid before they made this change that they would be entirely different, which could cause many more problems than it solved. They needn't have worried; they weren't completely changed. They kept many wonderful qualities.

There are those of us who fear "bad times." A few of us even hold ourselves back from success and the highs of life for fear

the lows will be even worse. The false belief is that if there are fewer highs, there will be fewer lows. Also, going from a high place to a low place feels worse than going from a low place to a lower place.

The reality is that *the difficult times of our lives are essential and are of the greatest value. The harder the times, the better!*

- The low times in our lives give us something to "push off of." If there were no bottoms in life to push off of, we could "drown" from the boredom in the middle strata of life.
- We learn from difficulty. Good times don't necessarily help us to learn anything. The "school of hard knocks" has been recognized for a very long time as the best school around.
- Without the lows of life, we'd have no real appreciation for the highs. Sweet tastes even better when we know what bitter is like.

So don't dread bad times and don't hold yourself back to try and avoid them. They happen anyway.

The fear some people have had about changing was based on the subconscious and incorrect assumption that they were altogether bad. They believed that if they got rid of what was "bad" about them, then everything had to go. In other words, *the lower the self-opinion a person has, the more he or she fears changing.*

Your last statement about not being able to find the switch to flip says to me that while you have some reservations and even some fear, you want to know how to go about making the change and you want to get on with it.

You said when you were reading books on how to be happy and more successful it was like being told to put one finger through a ring and then grab that finger and try to pull the rest of your body through. I guess I'm concerned it's going to be like that for me.

You may feel that way in part because you realize you have read a good deal of this book so far and you neither recall all you've read nor do you fully understand it. You may also doubt that you'll be able to completely understand and recall the remainder of this book.

Please be assured that you aren't required to understand or recall all that's here. Recommendations I'll make a little later will help you to further understand and to remember all that you need.

The *biggest obstacle to enjoying the benefits of what is here* is the "Do to Have to Be" perspective. You may think, "I'll read (Do) this book and learn (Have) more of what I need to know. Then I will enjoy greater success (Be) and consistently better moods (Be), free of damaging stress (Be)."

Unfortunately, with this way of thinking you can find yourself wondering, "But what if I'm not quite ready to do this? I'll put it off (procrastinate) for just a while until I am sure I'm ready for this." Or (unknown to you) you may think, "What if I don't take in (Do) the information well enough (perfectly) to get what I want? Then I'll feel even worse than before."

I strongly encourage you to learn about and benefit from what's here *because you deserve it*. You are worth it! You deserve the relief from stress, the success, the physical well-being, the good moods, and the more satisfying relationships.

Whatever it takes, I deserve it.

The Essence of What Is Needed to Be

Just how do I make the change to doing what I do and having what I have because I know I am worth it?

To become self-loving and self-accepting (in order to be all you want to be) you need to:

- *BE* aware
- *BE* truthful
- *BE* self-responsible
- *BE* in the here and now
- *BE*-lieve

This book will detail exactly how you go about fulfilling these needs. Right now I want to offer you a brief overview.

Be Aware

As children, we were given information and we interpreted happenings around us. Children don't have much experience or education and they have only part of the brain power (intelligence) they will have later, so as children we were easily influenced. We tended to believe blindly what we were told by word and by example.

Most of what we were told and our interpretations of our experiences were accurate and helpful. A simple illustration: "Be safe. Look both ways before you cross the street." We made accurate interpretations such as, "My brother climbed on the stove and got hurt. It is dangerous for me to climb on the stove, so I'll stay off it."

Unfortunately, some things we were told (and our interpretations) were entirely *inaccurate*. Some of those inaccuracies came to light and were changed over time. Others are maintained (we continue to believe them) and we may be totally unaware they are even present. A few false beliefs can become so entrenched and so central to our thinking that they influence much of what we do.

Sometimes I jokingly tell people with dangerous stress and other problems, "Your big mistake was that you were born way too young. If only you had waited until you were maybe 20 or so, you would have avoided most of those negative influences and inaccurate interpretations you made. And you wouldn't have all that hidden away in your mind making all this stress and problems. Of course, that would have been hard on your mother—carrying you for nine months and 20 years."

Here's a case in point. A while back, there was a popular book by Susan Forward and Joan Torres entitled *Men Who Hate Women*. A far more accurate title for the book would have been *Men Who Are Terrified By What They Think About Women*.

Some boys misinterpret the feelings and behaviors of adults (usually parents) to mean that women are highly threatening. (The father may have been unusually critical of the mother, or the mother may have been domineering.) The "threats" (women) are feared. At the same time, these boys learn that women are desirable. Later, as men, they want women and mistakenly believe them to be dangerous. These men use anger to "defend" themselves from women whom they most desire (usually their wives). The anger (typically in the form of sudden and irrational outbursts and strong criticism) is subconsciously intended to keep the woman emotionally off balance and therefore less of a "threat."

Actions and feelings based on inaccurate beliefs will be inaccurate.

Beliefs that may have been true, at least to some degree, when we were children may no longer be valid. As children, for example, we were cared for and looked after. Even strangers joined in the effort to help keep us from harm. Because we were children and unable to care for ourselves, others felt an obligation toward us.

Once we become adults, the vast majority of other people feel little obligation to help keep us out of trouble. If we expect that others will or "ought to" do so, we're apt to experience considerable grief.

David Burns, in his book *Feeling Good,* points out that thoughts or beliefs can happen "automatically"; they can occur in our mind when we're unaware of them. I'll give an example shortly.

What all this comes down to is this: inaccurate thoughts or beliefs are regularly marching through our mind and we are entirely unaware of them. *How stressed, successful, happy, and physically well we are absolutely depends on how many of those automatic thoughts we have and how farfetched they are.*

It's hard for me to believe that I'm thinking something and don't even know it. How can that be?

Imagine yourself riding in a car on a route that's familiar to you. You pass landmarks you easily recognize, and you think of what you need to get done later in the day. The radio plays in the background amid sounds of the car engine and traffic noises.

Curiously, you find yourself having feelings you haven't felt for years. Then you realize that the music on the radio was popular back when you had those feelings.

Without your realizing it, the music sparked subconscious thoughts—automatic thoughts—of years past and those thoughts (memories) generated the emotions.

In a similar way, inaccurate beliefs or thoughts formed in years past go on automatically in our mind and influence us negatively far more than we know. If we're to have any defense against these subconscious, automatic, negative thoughts, we desperately need to have awareness, to stop them and their sometimes tragic influence.

Be Truthful

Bringing automatic untruths to light is only a good start; we need to counteract them. And of course the best antidote for an untruth is the truth.

How can I know what the truth is?

That question brings us to the most amazing discovery I've made. It may be very difficult to believe, but please don't reject this idea. Test it out for yourself later, when you have the tools to do so.

The more you know the truth, the more you are free of excess stress—free of feelings such as anger, depression, guilt, and fear; free of obstacles or threats to your success; free of troubled relationships. If you have excess stress, or have hurtful feelings like guilt, or are not yet successful, or have troubled relationships, it is because you believe (most likely subconsciously) something that's not true or is based on an untruth.

The truth is considered by wise people to be the most important element in our lives. And an extremely worthwhile goal is to speak only the truth, to *ourselves*.

I am finding more and more that when I'm tense or in a "bad mood" I can simply tell myself: "I may not yet know what I'm thinking that accounts for this but no matter what it is, it's untrue." The result is that my degree of stress and my mood change for the better.

I'm totally convinced that excess stress and undesirable moods are the result of thinking something untrue.

Have you heard it said, "The truth hurts"? In fact, the truth doesn't hurt even a little. But fighting the truth is uncomfortable or even painful.

Test my discovery; I'm confident you'll experience the same beneficial effect. Later, I'll provide the means to recognize the truth easily in specific situations. Now I'd like to offer you several characteristics of truth.

- When you open yourself to the truth, you'll invariably like yourself better. You will be more unconditionally self-accepting and self-loving. You won't feel superior to others, but you won't feel inferior either.

- You will feel more no-matter-what loving of others. What others do or don't do will influence you negatively less and less. Yet you will find yourself more effectively getting what you need from personal and work relationships.

- When you know the truth, you will not *blame* anyone, including yourself, or anything else for how you feel, what you do or don't do, and what you have and don't have. Blaming, which is critical, will go out of your life. You'll avoid wasting your time fault-finding.

I'll clarify this last characteristic of truth as I explain what I mean about being self-responsible.

Be Self–Responsible

Victims of street crime typically blame themselves. They may not realize it, but they do.

"It's my fault I got mugged. I shouldn't have been taking a walk so late at night. I should have known better than to . . . ." The feelings resulting from their self-blaming are guilt and outwardly directed fear in the form of anger. They often have inwardly directed fear or anger, which generates depression.

Many therapists, in their efforts to help these victims, have assured them, "It's not your fault. There's no way you could have known someone would attack you."

The message to victims of crime is often, "You're not responsible."

Current research says that this kind of counseling may be more of a negative influence than a helpful therapy. Feeling they were not at fault, clients may continue doing what they had done before. They may tell themselves, "I shouldn't have to stay off the streets at night. I'm not doing anything wrong being there. So I'll go out there again." And they get mugged again.

We need to know that we can hold ourselves entirely responsible for what does and doesn't take place in our lives, without critically blaming ourselves. We can and very much need to be self-responsible rather than self-blaming. We can use our power to change what's going on rather than wallow in needless guilt, depression, and anger.

Being *self-responsible* means being oriented toward the possible (what you can do something about) instead of the impossible (what you are unable to do something about), being concerned with the here and now instead of with a past that is beyond changing or a future that isn't yet in need of your attention. For example, "The past is gone. I was mugged, and I can learn from it. Right now, I'm going to be responsible and take care of myself. I'll drive to the YMCA and take my walk there on the indoor track, where I'm safe."

Taking responsibility for yourself means avoiding blaming anyone or anything else for what you do now, have done, will do in the future; for what you have or haven't done; or for anything that happens to you.

When Judy and I married, she was used to cooking for six family members. Even though there were only two of us, she continued with six-person quantities. She didn't particularly like what she cooked, so what was I to do but try to eat it all? I couldn't hurt her feelings, could I?

Eating that much food and exercising very little back then, I soon added about 30 pounds of fat.

I blamed Judy for making me fat. I said she shouldn't have cooked so much food and she shouldn't have cooked food that was so fattening.

But Judy wasn't unhappy with how I looked. She loved me, and besides, she didn't think she was at fault for my stuffing my stomach full of fattening food even if she did cook it.

As long as I blamed Judy, or anyone or anything else, for my weight problem, I was going to stay fat, because I wasn't taking responsibility. I wasn't saying, "Okay self, we are responsible for having the fat. It's up to us to do something about it." Once I made that speech and took responsibility for having the fat, I changed the way I ate and exercised, got rid of all the added pounds, and kept them off.

Be in the Here and Now

Imagine you are on a path in a patch of shadowy woods. The path is clearly marked but there are dips and roots in it, and limbs have fallen onto it. The woods are filled with delicate flowers and ferns and other interesting sights that give you considerable pleasure. There are also predatory animals such as tigers that could harm you. But you have a durable and powerful flashlight. By keeping the beacon on the path near your feet you are able to step over and around obstacles in the path. The predators are frightened by the light and run away. You get to enjoy the flowers, ferns, and other wonderful things along the path. The more you keep your powerful light pointed near your feet, the safer and more easily you progress through the woods.

Occasionally you shine your light behind you, back down the path, or toward the path ahead. But you do that only briefly, to give yourself a sense of where you have been and where you are going; most of the time you keep your light steadily shining on the path at your feet. You're safe and you can enjoy the scenery. Sometimes you take out your compass and check it, to be sure you're going in the direction of your choice. You're on the right path, you are doing very well. Occasionally others on paths near yours walk with you, but you don't depend on their lights. You enjoy their company while they are there but you understand their need to use their lights for their own benefit.

The path in the woods illustrates living in the here and now— the only way to make it safely through life with as much stress-free enjoyment and productivity along the way as possible.

Some of us go down the path (life) shining our lights (focus of attention) too far and too frequently behind us (the past) and ahead of us (the future). We stumble (have needless stress and trouble) and miss much of the scenery (pleasures of life) along the way. We turn

off our lights (take less responsibility for ourselves) expecting that others will look out for us and shine their lights at our feet rather than taking care of themselves. We get upset with them when they don't and we fall. Usually we accuse them of not being fair to us.

This comment about "shining my light" behind me and further ahead—does that mean I shouldn't think of the past or the future?

A good question. What I mean is that it's in our best interest to spend relatively little time thinking of the past or future. When we stay in the present, we realize that the woods have a way of distorting the light. What we see is only an approximation of what will be or has been. We can get into serious trouble when we believe our memories of the past are accurate or when we think we can see the future. Guessing—even good guessing—isn't knowing what the future holds.

There's nothing wrong with doing some occasional looking ahead to plan and set goals. The danger is in doing it too often.

It's important, and not that difficult, to distinguish planning from shining your light ahead to the future in an inappropriate way. When you feel good-to-neutral, then you're planning. If you're thinking ahead and don't feel better from doing it, you're not planning or setting goals.

Life is far more than preparation for the "real thing." Right now is the real thing.

But I thought goal setting was supposed to be important. And here you're telling me not to do a lot of it. How come?

Having something you might call a "mission" to move toward and occasionally think about can give considerable relief of stress in the present, does no harm, and can be quite helpful in other ways. It's like checking your compass in the woods. We'll talk more about having a mission near the end of Chapter 7.

In my clinical practice, I talk with people who've taken trying to look to the future to an extreme. They've spent years in a job they hated, dreaming of the time they'd enjoy their retirement. When they retire they realize that most of their lives have already passed with little joy or satisfaction. With so little practice, they discover they don't even know how to be joyful and satisfied in their retirement.

When thoughts of the future or past interfere with your significant awareness of what's going on in the present, much harm is done.

Speaking of thoughts of the future, how'd you like to be as free of fears as is humanly possible? How would you like to have little, if any, fear of speaking in public or almost anything else?

I'd love it. But it doesn't sound possible. Can anyone actually be free of fear?

You can be free of fear as much as you can shine your light at your feet (live in the here and now). *Any time you are tense, apprehensive, afraid, or terrified you are most likely not living in the reality of your here and now.* At some level of your mind, you are pointing your light down your path somewhere.

It seems to me you are saying in effect, "Don't be afraid." That's easy to say. But you haven't told me how to manage it.

That's coming. Just stick with me.

A woman told me that soon after she began to practice what I'll be sharing with you, she had an interesting experience. She lived on a farm and one dark night she needed to go some distance from the house to get the truck. With her flashlight in hand, she walked along the rough dirt road, forcing herself to keep the light at her feet. At first she was afraid because by not shining the light around, she couldn't make sure there were no ghosts out there.

She laughed and said, "I don't know what I thought I'd have done if there *were* ghosts there. I did make it to the truck without stumbling and without getting off the road. It was a good lesson for me."

Keep your light at your feet and take your life, and this book, one sure step at a time. You can do it.

Believe

To live life forward you need to believe the truths you're told. When you believe something, that means you think something, and your thinking is supported by your feelings. You'll act, when you believe.

I told you earlier that you probably (and most likely do) have hidden stress that's a danger to you. It isn't what happens to you or around you that stresses you or gives you bad moods, it's what you *think*—thoughts that happen so quickly or deeply that you don't even recognize them. Stress from traffic and similar sources is an illusion. You may accept what I'm telling you as absolutely true— after all, I and others have studied stress for many years and you haven't—but you need to *believe* what I'm telling you, for it to benefit you. I want that benefit for you. I very much want the help I'm offering in this book to help you a great deal.

So if I only think what you're saying is fact, that's not enough because I won't do enough of what I need to do to get rid of my stress and moods. Then how do I get to believe you?

As I said before, much of what's here was in a text I wrote for my family, my friends, and many of my clients. After *some* of them read the material, they said in so many words, "But I don't feel any better." When I asked if they were regularly doing, or doing at all, what I strongly recommended in the text, they would say, again in so many words, "Why, no. Do you think that would help?"

I know of no way to bypass doing. *It takes at least some doing to believe.* Try some of the suggestions for changing your stress-promoting thinking, in order to believe enough to keep on doing them.

Now, I want . . .

Wait. Are you going to tell about something else?

Yes, I was going to talk about our ways of thinking (that we don't know about) that create stress.

Before you get into that, I want to know something. You made a comment a little while ago about there being two kinds of self-esteem: what we know about and what we don't know about. You said the kind we don't know about is the more important one. Tell me more.

I admire your interest in learning about the self-esteem we don't realize is there which I call secret self-esteem; many people would rather not know any secrets about themselves. Your question is a good sign. What you want to learn will take a little while to explain and you'll need to respond to an inventory that could take you 10 or 15 minutes to do. The time will be well worth it, though. Understanding about secret self-esteem can help you gain considerable protection from negative stress in the future.

Go ahead then. I want all the protection I can get.

4

Your Secret
Self-Esteem

*The Self-Esteem You Don't Know
about That Matters the Most*

My observations, experience, and study have convinced me that, whether or not they realize it, *people will sooner or later see to it that their lives turn out according to how they feel about themselves down deep* (their secret self-esteem). People can and often do make life exceedingly difficult and highly stressful for themselves, yet they're entirely unaware they're doing it. I call this situation the "duck roast." Remember the experiment described on page 14, with a duck in hot water. For some people, their duck roast is a messed-up career. For others it's separation from their spouse and their family. For many it's a severe illness. For still others it's a "mental breakdown." Duck roasts vary from person to person.

Here's an example. Someone I'll call Wesley grew up poor. He got only one pair of shoes a year, and was given those when school began so they'd last until warm weather. Wesley would tell himself, "One day, I'll have money." (Something he already had as a child, and didn't know it, was a hurt secret self-esteem.) I suspect he

equated a person's value with how much money the person had; the more money, the better the person.

With a good deal of hard work and initiative, Wesley managed, as a young adult, to buy a small hardware store. Over the years, he made wise decisions, put in long hours, and made the store highly successful. His family became one of the wealthiest in his community.

Within a few years of a well-deserved retirement, Wesley was approached by a younger man who had several ideas about how the store could be made more profitable. The newcomer had some corporate experience, was confident, and spoke with much authority. He had practically no experience in retail selling, but that didn't seem to matter.

At least it didn't matter to Wesley. It did mean something to his family. They were leery of the stranger and they let their thoughts and feelings be known. The family was concerned that Wesley was being taken in by this newcomer, especially when he let him manage the store.

Within a couple of years, the business that had once been a model of success was on the brink of financial disaster. Family and friends were finally able to make Wesley see what was happening. Had he refused to recognize what was obvious to so many others, in a short while it would've been too late. He would have roasted his duck to well-done.

To find out how likely you are to smell a duck roasting, take the self-esteem inventory on pages 59–63. Don't go past it and read more. Your self-test is important to your understanding.

Lovelace Secret and Surface Self-Esteem Inventory

Directions: To select from each of the 20 parts, write down the column letter (A, B, or C) of the statement that *best describes* you. Space requirements have limited the possible descriptions; perhaps only a few of the descriptions will fit you exactly. In some parts, more than one statement might be valid. *Pick the one that comes the closest to describing you.* Avoid responding with what you believe are the "right" answers. *All answers are right when you give the most accurate responses you can.* Write down only one letter in each fill-in space or on a separate sheet of paper, and don't skip any numbered items.

	A	**B**	**C**
1.	When someone says something bad about me, it doesn't really affect me. Or, I like it when someone is bothered by what I do or say.	My feelings are hurt by someone's disapproval of me or of what I do or say.	Someone's criticism of me, if anything, increases my caring about or understanding of the person criticizing me.
2.	I feel I'm able to control what someone does or doesn't do, or control how he or she feels. And I seem to need that.	Too often I feel out of control or powerless. Or I feel manipulated.	I understand that I am in control of myself. No one can control me. And I have little interest in trying to control anyone else.
3.	If anything, I think of myself as being better than other people.	I think of myself as being less important than other people.	I understand and behave like I'm no better or worse than anyone else.
4.	How I look is very important to me. If possible, I want to always look my best and be in fashion.	I don't care that much how I look as long as I'm comfortable and clean.	How I look is important to the degree I want it to reflect how good I feel about myself. (My body is *now* adequately lean and fit and I am usually well groomed and clean.)

	A	**B**	**C**
___ 5.	Actually, I don't mind a good argument. It helps to clear the air or makes life more interesting.	I dislike a fight or argument. And I'll do what I can to avoid it.	I don't try to avoid arguments—they are all right with me. Still, I don't try to win them at other people's expense.
___ 6.	I don't really care about helping other people. I easily turn down nearly all requests for help.	It's about impossible for me to turn down a genuine plea for help.	I help others and I help myself. I won't help others if it means doing harm to myself. I may regularly turn people down.
___ 7.	I believe, or others tell me, I'm a perfectionist. I'm *not* likely to be satisfied until most things are done and done well.	Often I don't care if most things get done or how well they are done. It just isn't that important to me.	I do what I do well because I deserve it. And if I don't do well, I'm rarely bothered at all.
___ 8.	I dislike making mistakes and avoid them whenever possible.	Too often, my life seems to be filled with mistakes. I don't seem to be able to avoid them for long.	I don't usually make mistakes, but when I do I'm not upset much.
___ 9.	If at all possible I don't ask for help. I feel I should be able to do without it.	I ask for help and don't mind it that much. Still, too often it doesn't work that well.	I usually know when I need help, and I ask for it. If the help doesn't fit, I can often get it to work.
___ 10.	I regularly criticize other people and situations. Maybe I shouldn't, but it helps to let it out.	I was taught it wasn't right to criticize, so I avoid it as much as I can. Maybe I do hold it inside.	I'm rarely critical and not because it isn't proper. It's more that my mind doesn't work that way.

A	**B**	**C**
_____ 11. If someone disagrees with me, I think he or she just has a different opinion. That's okay.	If someone challenges what I believe is true, I more than likely assume I'm wrong. I'll probably change my mind.	If someone challenges what I believe is true, more than likely I think they are wrong. And I want to convince them to think my way.
_____ 12. I'm comfortable with praise, but I don't really need it to feel good about myself and what I do.	I need recognition. Most everyone needs praise for the good they do or for what they accomplish.	I don't much care if I get praised or not. In fact, I tend to feel uncomfortable being fussed over.
_____ 13. It just doesn't normally occur to me to pay attention to who likes me and doesn't or how many friends I have.	Not many people like me. Or the ones who do like me I don't care for that much.	I have (or hope I have) many friends and keeping those relationships is very important.
_____ 14. Material goods or success comes to me as a kind of byproduct of living my life happily.	I don't much care about getting ahead. It's just more to keep up with and be concerned about.	Getting ahead in life—career success or having valuable things (or success as a homemaker)—is important to me. And I'm working hard for it.
_____ 15. I'm normally too busy enjoying or learning from what's going on now to think or talk about past accomplishments.	There isn't that much I have to be proud of. Or there is and I keep it to myself because it isn't right to brag.	At times anyway, I'm quick to let others know about what I've accomplished or the good things that happen to me. I'm not real shy about singing my own praises.

	A	**B**	**C**
___ 16.	I'm entirely responsible for what happens in my life. Blaming others or circumstances doesn't make any more sense than feeling badly about the past you aren't able to change.	Many of the bad things that happen to me are my fault. I feel guilty about or regret such mistakes.	If things go wrong, it usually isn't my fault. Other people or circumstances are probably to blame.
___ 17.	There is a sense of positive direction to my life that somehow comes more out of my great worth as a person than out of goals I set and reach.	There seems to be little to no direction to my life. It's hard to imagine things getting to be good for me.	I often do (or think I should) set goals or objectives and evaluate my progress in attaining them. If life gets tough, I can think about how good it can be some day.
___ 18.	My usual manner could best be described as "happy." When needed, I easily speak up for myself without being harsh. I do confront well.	I'm usually reserved. I don't speak harshly to others and try always to be considerate, even if it means my needs go unmet. I don't confront all that well.	I have something of a blunt or brusque manner. I'm rather outspoken and it sometimes comes across to others as "mean" or "aggressive."
___ 19.	Whether "fair" or not, people do what they believe is in their best interest. I don't think that's wrong. It's just how people are.	Most people look out for themselves and will pretty much do whatever they think they can get away with. It's not right, but it's how people are.	I have definite beliefs about what is and is not fair. And I'm upset when I or others are treated unfairly.
___ 20.	I know that what others say will not hurt me. It's only what I say that hurts me.	I am careful about what I say, because I might hurt someone else.	I am careful about what I say, because someone might use it to hurt me.

_____ 21. Write down the number below that best describes how you *now* feel about yourself. The 1 at one extreme stands for absolutely hating yourself. The 7 at the other extreme stands for the very best you can possibly feel about yourself. Perhaps a number in between the two extremes better describes how you now feel about yourself. Please write or circle a number now.

Totally Hate Myself						**Totally Love Myself**
1	2	3	4	5	6	7

Now that I've written the 20 letters and one number, how do I find out what they mean?

To score the inventory you first go to item 11. Beginning with item 11, each A you wrote needs to be changed to a C. Starting with item 11, each C you wrote needs to be changed to an A. Now count and write down the number of As you wrote, the number of Bs, and the number of Cs.

Why did you ask me to change the letters, starting with item 11?

To help assure that you get a more accurate indication of what your secret self-esteem is like. But do keep in mind that no attitudinal or behavioral inventory (including this one or any other I know of) tells you absolute facts. Inventories only indicate possibilities for you to consider. If the results are helpful and make sense, then use them.

The more Cs you recorded, the stronger your secret self-esteem (what you think of yourself beneath the surface). The number you wrote in response to item 21 represents your surface self-esteem (what you think of yourself consciously). If you wrote the number four, then your surface self-esteem is about average, compared to how you believe most people think of themselves.

So what do these numbers mean?

If the number you wrote in response to item 21 was *less than four,* some work on your self-esteem can help to insure progress in staying free of negative stress. If you had *fewer than 11 C answers* on the first 20 items, working to strengthen your self-esteem is even more important. Fewer than 11 C answers indicates that how you feel about yourself beneath the surface is suffering. Your self-description needs and deserves your attention, to help protect yourself from career- and life-threatening stress.

The Aggressive Type

Provided you had fewer than 11 C responses, the more A answers you gave, particularly if more than 8, the more you have hurt secret self-esteem. I would describe your secret self-esteem as the "aggressive type." You tend toward perfectionistic behavior and are critical of one or more others. You are likely to place considerable emphasis on achieving recognition and "getting ahead" in your career, in business or at home. You probably won't recognize that you have hurt self-esteem. Your pushiness, in part, is an attempt to keep the awareness of hurt self-esteem from yourself. Chances are, you gave yourself a 4 or more on item 21. You're not as likely to recognize your higher level of stress and discomfort.

Because you have more A answers, you probably give an appearance of self-confidence. All the while, you have hidden self-doubts. You have a tendency to build up anger and you're likely to speak up in defense of your rights. Also, you're inclined to give others reason to worry or agonize, rather than worry or agonize yourself.

When and if you do a duck roast with stress, it's more likely to be or seem to be faster and to occur later in life. You'll have a good deal of success but you'll throw it away or you'll shoot yourself in the foot soon after or just before you really "make it."

The Passive Type

With fewer than 11 C answers, the more B descriptive statements you chose, especially if 7 or more, the more you have hurt secret self-esteem. Yours is the "passive type." Chances are, you appear to be mildly perfectionistic. You're less critical of others than you are of yourself, but you can sometimes be highly critical of others. You have a low level of concern with outward signs of financial and social success. You're likely to recognize that you too often don't feel good about yourself and that you have a problem with stress. You more likely feel hurt, sad, or fearful rather than angry. Only occasionally will you speak up for yourself when others ignore your needs.

Chances are, you worry a lot or you tend to agonize over past events, even those that took place years ago. You're likely to do a slow roast with stress. Instead of committing health, career, or social suicide later in life, you're apt to experience smaller but significant difficulties spaced out over your lifetime.

If you had 11 or fewer C responses and about equal numbers of A and B responses, then you're neither clearly aggressive nor clearly passive with regard to hurt secret self-esteem. You're more likely to show a mixture of characteristics typical of those higher in A or B responses. Whether you realize it or not, your level of stress is probably too high and in need of reducing. As much as anyone else, you need to build your self-concept.

Strong Secret Self-Esteem

If you scored 11 to 16 C responses, you're among those identified as having strong secret self-esteem; you're doing better than most people in keeping stress and hurtful moods in hand. You're at less risk for a duck roast. You already possess many of the attitudes this book encourages. And you're likely to find here a good deal of confirmation and strength to proceed as you are.

You didn't say what it means if someone scores more than 16 C responses.

So far, almost no one, including myself, has given more than 16 C answers. My educated guess is that anyone who scores more than 16 C's is telling more about how they know they need to feel and behave than about what's actually going on inside them.

Then they're kidding themselves?

Probably they are.

Some Background

I didn't want to give much background on the inventory of secret and surface self-esteem until you had a chance to use and score it; I might have decreased its value to you. Let me give that background now.

My reading and study have more often identified for me the signs of hurt self-concept than the indications of strong self-esteem.

I'm not sure what you mean by that.

When I talk to people who know about self-esteem or read what they've written, I find that they concentrate heavily on signs of damaged or low self-esteem. The following are some examples of what is typically said about those who have low self-esteem:

- Put themselves down a good deal.
- Readily interpret behavior of others as showing lack of love or respect.
- Have extramarital affairs.
- Tend to be critical or condemning of others.
- Complain a good deal about health, job, and so on.
- Make fun of others.
- Have a strong need for recognition or praise from other people.
- Insist that there are two ways of doing things: their way and the wrong way.
- Are reluctant to try new things or to advance economically or socially.
- Are more apt to use illegal drugs.
- Are more apt to abuse humans and animals.
- Are more apt to commit criminal acts.
- Achieve poor performance in school, when they could do well.
- Are regularly afraid, angry, or depressed.
- Feel consumed with "getting ahead" financially or socially.
- Have significant excess fat or an unkempt appearance.
- Are overly concerned about appearance.
- Feel controlled or manipulated by others.
- Want to control others.

Over the years, I have talked with many people, including friends and clients, who seemed sincere when they said they felt good about themselves. I sensed that they didn't, and their actions—extramarital affairs, legal trouble, and excessive drinking—said to me that they didn't like themselves as much as they said they did. I was convinced that how a person feels about himself or herself is associated with obvious and hidden stress. The more you like you, the less stress you're likely to experience no matter what happens around you or to you.

Increasingly, I wanted to find out if I could develop an inventory that would get at the deep-down sense of self-worth I thought was there. I asked myself, "What do people do or think that indicates to me that they genuinely like themselves? What do other experts in the field of self-development and personal growth say points to a good sense of self-worth?" Finally, and most important, I asked, "What are some key ways of thinking that I identify as indicating high self-esteem?"

With the answers to the preceding questions, I put together the original inventory. Over the course of several months, I gave the inventory to people I knew well, and then reworked and rewrote it many times based on their responses.

Once I had a finalized form of the inventory I gave it to many of my clients and acquaintances. From the data I collected I can make statements to you about your results.

From the data I learned:

- The more stress, hidden or obvious, a person had, the lower he or she tended to score in self-esteem.
- Many people indicated that they thought they had at least average self-esteem (a score of 4 on the last item of the self-esteem inventory). Yet they scored less than that on the remainder of the inventory.
- Hurt secret self-esteem takes two distinct forms: aggressive and passive. I've already described both to you.
- Surface self-esteem can easily change from day to day because it's sensitive to surroundings. On a good day it's higher. Secret self-esteem is far more important, more stable, and not influenced by good days or bad days. It changes slowly, in response to the quality of thinking.

Is there anything else I need to understand about duck roasting or about my scores on the inventory I took?

Yes, several things:

- If you gave no C response, you aren't at all inferior to someone who gave 20 C responses. This inventory is not a test of your value. It's an indicator of what you think (both secretly and on the surface) your value is. *The reality is that you are of great value, no matter how you feel about yourself.*

- If you're disappointed about how you did on the inventory, then you don't yet understand its purpose. Your reaction can help you recognize that you tend to live life backward. You mistakenly believe your value depends on how well you Do or what you Have. "If I do well on the inventory and have a lot of 'good' answers, then I am a good person. Otherwise, I'm not." Not true! You need to live life forward.

- What you *think* you think of yourself consciously can be different from what you actually think of yourself at a deeper level. Knowing how well you like yourself down deep decides many crucial aspects of your life including how much stress you'll have on a day-to-day basis or will ultimately experience.

- It's entirely within your power to alter, for the better, your self-concept at all levels. You can then positively affect your stress level and your moods.

How's that done?

The way you change how you feel about yourself and your level of stress is to change how you think.

But isn't how I think awfully set in my mind? It isn't like changing my shoes, you know.

I and many others have done it. You can too.

5

Major Mallard
Mutterings

Prominent Ways of Thinking That
Cause Your Negative Stress

I'm absolutely convinced that 27 faulty ways of thinking cause nearly 100 percent of excess stress (the kind this book is about). They also cause almost all of the anger, fear, jealousy, worry, hurt feelings, depression, nervousness, envy, disappointment, frustration, guilt, feelings of inferiority, insecurity, loneliness, prejudice, divorce and poor relationships, self-pity, violence, lack of success, and drug addiction in the world. These thoughts also account for much of the poor physical well-being and mental illness on our planet. We'll discuss all 27 of them in this chapter and Chapter 6. These are the names I've given them:

1. "Makes me feel" thinking
2. "Makes me do" thinking
3. Oughty thoughts
4. "It's not fair" thinking
5. "Making magic" thinking

6. "Can't" thinking
7. "I just know" thinking
8. "Grate expectations" thinking
9. Faulty thinking—placing blame
10. "Don't like" thinking
11. "What people say matters most" thinking
12. "Get even" thinking
13. "Always/never" thinking
14. "If only" thinking
15. "I can make up for" thinking
16. "I'm my shirt" thinking
17. Hindsight-labels thinking
18. "Terrible" thinking
19. "Yes, but" thinking
20. "Don't" thinking
21. "I'll do better when" thinking
22. "Poor me" thinking
23. Duck-plays-ostrich thinking
24. "Luck" (sounds like duck) thinking
25. "It's too hard" thinking
26. "Lost" thinking
27. Racy thinking

To the degree we're able to be free of these 27 incorrect ways of thinking, we'll be free of excess negative stress. We will be successful and happy, have good and lasting relationships, and be far more likely to have excellent physical and mental well-being.

Faulty thoughts violate one and usually more of the Be's we talked about in Chapter 3—Be aware, Be truthful, Be responsible,

Be in the here and now, Be-lieve. They thrive on being unaware, untruthful, irresponsible, in any era but the present, and unbelieving. None of them is truthful. They are lies.

We'll examine some of the more common of those untruths in this chapter.

Duck and Eagle Thinking

For many years I've heard managers in business firms say, "Don't send your ducks to eagle school," expressing the belief that there are eagle-type people and duck-type people. The eagle types are those with the greatest potential for doing a good job in management. Only eagle types are sent for training as leaders.

Duck types rarely get off the ground and spend a lot of time making noise and going around in circles and nowhere in particular. They try to avoid responsibility and rigidly stick with what is familiar. The eagle types soar to great heights, go far, and thoroughly enjoy life.

A psychotherapist and public speaker I enjoy listening to had also heard the quote about not sending ducks to eagle school. During a lecture he was giving to a large group of business people, I heard him say, "Some people are ducks and others are eagles. It's exceedingly difficult to get them to change. And there are many more ducks than eagles." He went on to give some examples of experiences he had had with individuals he considered to be ducks and others he thought were eagles. Finally, he indicated that the job of an employer was to look for and hire eagles—those who would learn well and do a good job.

My reaction to this part of the lecture was, "People aren't ducks or eagles. Some think like ducks in the sense that how they think hurts themselves, their performance, and their ability to succeed. People aren't naturally that way and certainly don't have to stay that way. They change to perform better and succeed, by altering the way they think." It then occurred to me that the duck and eagle descriptions were already familiar to many people. So, I've continued to use them.

When we rely on inaccurate thoughts that send us in circles to make the same mistakes over and over again, we're thinking like ducks. To whatever degree we're thinking thoughts that are true and promote success, love of ourselves, and love of others, we are thinking as eagles. Let's think eagle thoughts!

Then what you're saying is that using the words duck and eagle is a handy way to describe particular ways of thinking. Duck-like thinking describes thinking that's untrue and won't get you very far in life or keep you there. Eagle-like thinking is accurate and helps you to "fly" and make good progress.

That's close enough to what I'm talking about. You can add that thinking as an eagle leads to far less dangerous stress and promotes better moods.

But is duck-like thinking wrong?

No—not at all. One of the aspects I appreciate about this approach is that in real life the ducks and eagles aren't normally judged as being right or wrong or as superior and inferior. Ducks and eagles are similar in some ways but clearly different in others. A person isn't bad or wrong for doing duck-like thinking. People don't choose how they think. They pick it up when they're young, when they don't know any better.

Really, everything depends on how you *want* to live your life. Realizing that duck-like thinking will lead to needless stress, emotional trouble, hurt relationships, career problems, and poor health, most people will choose to learn about and do more and more eagle-like thinking. My goal is to offer you that choice.

Duck-like thinking says nothing about your level of intelligence. Very bright people are as likely to be duck thinkers as those who are less intelligent.

"Makes Me Feel" Thinking

Let's begin with the duck thought that is perhaps the biggest falsehood and creates much needless pain. The other untruths are important but if you fully understand, accept, and make use of this one, you will have made wonderful progress toward being a stress master.

I occasionally say to people, "I've discovered you are from Mars." As sincerely as I can, I go on to tell these people I've been told that they were sent here to find out Earth's secrets and to take those secrets back to their fellow Martians. Still further, in the process of spying on Earth they have destroyed countless numbers of innocent insects, mostly ants and beetles.

By this time the people I'm telling this to have a half-smile on their face. When I ask them why they aren't upset at my calling them a Martian, a spy (stealing Earth's secrets), and a murderer (killing ants and beetles), they begin with a superficial reason such as, "I didn't think you were serious." I then ask them, "Would you be upset if you thought that I *was* serious, if I actually thought that you were from Mars?" Most people reply, "I wouldn't have been upset by that."

"Why not?"

"Because it isn't *true* that I'm from Mars."

I'm not sure I understand what you mean.

The point is—and this is very important—*what you and I believe is true determines what we feel and how much hurtful stress we have.* The cause of our feelings and stress is inside us and we identify it as reality.

We may often make comments such as, "He made me so angry." "The office was depressing (made me depressed)." "Johnny hurt my feelings." "She made me feel so loved." "My job is so stressful." But they simply are not true statements!

So, "makes me feel" thinking not only violates the Be truthful criterion described earlier; it also goes against the Be aware and Be responsible premises. When we say or think that someone else or something else determines what we feel (what our emotions are) we're being unaware of the facts. We're also denying our responsibility for our feelings. Being responsible for what we feel means we can change any feeling that gets in our way.

Self-responsibility means self-control.

You say that situations, places, and people don't make me feel anything or cause my stress; that it's what I think is true or not true that decides those reactions. Then how come I feel stress or anger if someone calls me a bad name?

If someone calls you an SOB and you don't yet know you aren't an SOB, then you are going to be upset about it. Realize it or not, you believe you've been found out. (This is hurt secret self-esteem.) Once you know you aren't an SOB, rather than being upset at being labeled one, you'll most likely wonder what the other person's problem is, why he or she is making such an error. You may be curious or even concerned for the name-caller, but you won't be angry or stressed.

Just a minute. Are you saying I should let people get away with saying anything they want to me, even calling me an SOB?

If someone is upset and calls you an SOB or anything else, or criticizes you, but you're genuinely confident and at ease, why would you want to retaliate? The other person is already at a considerable disadvantage: you're much better off than he or she is.

Besides, if you get upset over being called an SOB or anything else—maybe a lazy bum, a creep, a whore, a nerd, a bitch—then that means you (down deep) don't yet know you aren't what you've been called. When you get upset at accusations, you're subtly giving back the message that you think they may be correct. I don't believe you want to give that message.

Remember too, no one can make us *think* something and no one can make us feel something. What we think comes from our memories and our interpretations of what is going on and has happened. You and I are the ultimate sources of what we think. To deny that responsibility is to deny our considerable value and power.

Let's review the key points on "makes me feel" thinking that we've covered so far.

- We create our own feelings based on what we believe to be reality.
- If we are under excess stress or upset, it's because we believe something that is untrue or is based on untruth.
- Nearly all of the excess stress, worry, fear, and anger we experience is caused by incorrect beliefs and misconceptions, not by what's going on around us or by what others say or do.

A woman once told me she couldn't "buy" my assertion that if she hurt, it wasn't because of what someone else did but because she believed an untruth to be reality. She reminded me that her husband had had a "one-night stand" with a former girlfriend. *That* was the truth; that "fact" had caused her upset. She was devastated by his volunteering the information to her in a "fit of honesty."

I told her that I didn't believe it was her husband's admission of infidelity that was upsetting her, but what she was telling herself in response to it. His misdeed said something to her about herself that was anything but a compliment. She thought the reality was that something was wrong with her, that if she were the person or wife she should have been, he would not have fooled around. But that simply was not true.

The fact was, I said, her husband's behavior said a great deal about the "duckiness" of his thinking. He was trying to improve how he felt about himself through an illicit sexual encounter, which rarely, if ever, works.

Duck thinking produces duck feelings. When thinking is false, the feelings produced by that thinking are also false.

I reminded her that her husband had volunteered the information about his misbehavior, regretted it, and revealed it even though he hadn't been caught, which likely meant he would not do it again. People who are apt to repeat such behavior rarely (it seems to me) confess unless they are caught or after just one encounter. She logically had reason to feel good about that.

We express "makes me feel" thinking in many ways. Here are just some of them:

". . . makes me so sad."

". . . hurt my feelings."

". . . got so upset when she heard . . ."

". . . gets on my nerves."

"I was terribly jealous when he . . ."

"My heart was broken when she wrote that . . ."

"It was a heart-wrenching ordeal."

". . . makes me so crazy."

"This is the most boring . . ."

". . . gets my goat."

"I feel so safe when he . . ."

"My boss is always on my back about . . ."
"This is such a high-pressure job."

———————

"Makes Me Do" Thinking

When you're telling yourself, probably subconsciously or without realizing it, that you *must* or *have to* do something, I sometimes call that "mind in the gotta" thinking. "I've just gotta make a good impression on . . . ." "I *must* pass this test." "I *have to* pick up the kids at 2:30 this afternoon."

When I ask people to list some of the activities they might tell themselves they *have to* do each day, I hear comments like:

"I have to get up in the morning."
"I have to get ready for work (or school)."
"I must get to work (or school) on time."
"I've got to keep the house (or yard) at least fairly clean."

But don't you think most people tell themselves they *have to* do these kinds of things?

Words and phrases such as "gotta, makes me, must, have to" literally mean there's no option; there's absolutely no alternative. And the fact is that there are alternatives. You don't have to get up, go to work, get to work on time, clean the house, or anything else. No one and no situation makes you do anything. You have the option—even if it's unacceptable—of staying in bed, and so on.

———————

In dealing with children, it can help to let them know they have choices, while still influencing their actions. For example, instead of saying, "You *have to* go to Grandma's!" you might ask the child, "Would you like to go to Grandma's house the long way and see the geese in the pond, or go the short way?"

———————

Whenever we say, "I've gotta" we are violating the Be's I've described before that are essential to self-acceptance and self-love. Remember, self-love and self-acceptance are essential to stress mastery and all it brings.

The first Be it violates is Be truthful. It simply isn't a fact that we have no options, that we must or have to do something.

It may not be exactly true, but I know what I mean when I say I have to do something. I know I have options. It's just a way of expressing something. So what's the big deal?

It may be a fact that your conscious mind knows it's just an expression, even if it's untrue. The major trouble is, your subconscious mind, which hears such comments, takes it literally. Your subconscious mind actually thinks you have no choice, and the implication is clear: You're weak and inferior. All other people have choices, but you don't. Every time you say you *have* to do something, you are giving your subconscious a message that increases internal feelings of inferiority! All those "gotta's" add up over the years and you pay a very dear price for them whether you know it or believe it or not. My friend, you deserve far better!

The second Be that's violated is Be responsible. By saying, "I have to" you're denying your responsibility. "Someone or something else is making me do a particular thing. I don't have any choice." That's just not reality.

If it isn't reality, then how do we get to thinking this way?

We learn to "put our minds in the gotta" as children, when parents and others tell us we "have to" do things. For example, "You're going to *have to* take your brother with you to the movies." "You *must* not talk in church." Parents and other adults don't want children to realize they have choices. If they did, they might fight the adults' wishes and do something other than what is wanted. It's easier on adults for children to think of themselves as not having options other than doing what they're told.

So what you are saying is, it's my parents' and teachers' fault that I unwittingly hurt myself by saying that I have to do stuff.

While you and I deserve no criticism for it—after all, we were young and didn't know any better—you and I believed and accepted what we were told. It's ultimately our responsibility and not our parents' or teachers' or anyone else's.

What's the advantage of taking this responsibility and saying that we do all that we do by our own obvious or hidden choices and not because we're made to?

The great value of accepting responsibility is that we have the option to change. If someone else or something else were responsible, we would need to wait for that person or situation to change. And that could be never.

A major universal challenge is that we learned to think as children from people who also learned to think when they were children. The passing along of duck thoughts from generation to generation was insured.

Some of the ways we learn to say "makes me do" are:

"I just have to . . . ."

"I must do it."

". . . pulls my strings."

". . . pushes my buttons."

"I've gotta know."

"That causes me to . . . ."

"She made me do it."

"I had better do this."

Oughty Thoughts

What I call "oughty thoughts" typically include words such as "should, shouldn't, ought to, and ought not to." These are words we associate with parents or parent-like people (teachers, grandparents, police, etc.). These "authority figures" regularly make comments such as, "You *should* go to bed early." "You *shouldn't* talk back to grownups." "You *ought to* appreciate what others give you."

"Oughty talk" implies that the speaker knows about definite rules or guidelines to be obeyed. It implies that either we're ignorant of them, or we know them but are disobeying them. The basic idea in such "oughty talk" is to try to control and direct our behavior in a way that may or may not be in our best interest, but is believed to be in the best interest of whoever is using the "oughts" and "shoulds."

As children, we hear this kind of talk from parent figures and other children acting as parents. We incorporate the words into our vocabulary and begin to think oughty thoughts directed toward others and ourselves such as, "She shouldn't treat me that way." Many problems with "oughty thinking" make it extremely important to avoid. I'll mention just some of them. First, statements that include words like "should" or "ought" are often untrue. For example, there are no universally decreed rules that say children cannot "talk back" to—challenge the authority—of grownups. And where is it written that you are required to appreciate what others do for you?

Hold on, are you saying that I *shouldn't*—I mean I don't need to—appreciate what others do for me?

In many cases, it may well be in your best interest to avoid challenging authority and to show appreciation to others. My point is that they're not required of you, and shoulds and oughts imply that they are.

Besides not being factual, oughty thoughts and oughty talk are often intended to control or manipulate. The controlling factor is the feeling of *guilt*. We cause ourselves to feel guilt when we don't do what we or others tell ourselves we should or shouldn't do.

There's a fanciful "love story" I want you to hear; it illustrates how complicated oughty thoughts and guilt can be. About 100 years ago in a small town in Europe, a young man who was poor and had a severely bent back was in love with the mayor's daughter. Realizing that the girl was approaching the age when she would be married, he went to her father and told him he wanted to court his daughter. The mayor said he doubted that his daughter, a beautiful and wealthy young woman with many prospective suitors, would be interested in him. The young man pleaded for the opportunity to at least talk briefly with the girl. Feeling sorry for the young man and thinking it would do no harm, the father consented to a brief meeting the following day in the family's parlor.

The young man arrived early and waited nervously. The mayor's daughter remembered the suitor only because of his badly deformed back. After a bit of small talk, the young man told the girl, "As you know, we have a legend that says that just before we are born an angel calls out the name of the person we will marry." Most people forget the name of their intended but, he said, he had remembered and the name was that of the mayor's daughter. The angel had also said that the person he was going to marry would have a severely bent spine. He told the girl he had begged the angel to allow him to bear the misfortune for his wife-to-be, and his wish was granted.

The implications were that the young man had made a great sacrifice for this beautiful young woman and that it was the will of God that she marry him. Believing this to be true, the girl told herself, "I *should* be grateful to this person. He has done so much for me, I owe him my hand in marriage." She soon agreed to marry him.

When I first heard this story, my reaction was, "That was a mean thing for the young man to do. He manipulated that girl with guilt. Perhaps she married him and spent many years with someone she didn't love, who depended on her family financially."

Then I realized that the responsibility was with the girl. The young man's "oughty" thinking and talk hadn't led to the acceptance of his proposal. Her should-y thinking or oughty thoughts were responsible. She believed stories that were untrue (his conversation with the angel) and because she believed them, she suffered guilt and allowed herself to be manipulated.

I still don't think it was fair for the guy to trick her that way.

That's what I call "it's not fair" thinking.

"It's Not Fair" Thinking

"Play fair! Daddy, John isn't playing fair. He moved his Monopoly piece three times and he was only supposed to move it two times." Statements like this might have been ours as children, and we still hear children say them.

As children, we do much of our learning, to prepare for adult life, through playing games. We learn to cooperate and to control our impulses.

Unfortunately, we, as children and later as adults, come to believe that life itself is a game and somehow we are players. But life isn't a game! Life is real. And while games have rules and an expectation that those who play will always obey the rules (play fair), life is not that way. *If we think life is a game to be played fairly, we're at a considerable disadvantage to those who know better.*

Sometimes I ask people, "Do you know what's truly fair?" Then I answer my own question: "The place where they have the ferris wheel. That's what fair is."

What you and I can truly count on in life is that nature, our situation, government, and other people will not treat us "fairly," but in ways that are believed to be in their best interest. Much of the time, their interests will also work out for us—but not always.

Both duck-like thinkers and eagle-like thinkers do what they believe is in their best interest. The difference is that eagle-like thinkers are much more apt to be right. What they do is in their best interest and is respectful of the legitimate needs of others.

I see many couples in marital therapy saying in all kinds of ways, "He (or she) doesn't treat me fairly and should." They tell how their spouses don't do a "fair share" of the housework, or don't want sex often enough. They are getting all grades of upset about it and their marriages are at the brink of destruction—all because they maintain their childhood belief that life is fair and others should treat them fairly.

Once marital partners or anyone else accept that their insistence on being treated fairly is based on a childhood misconception of reality, they can move beyond needless hurt feelings—they are better masters of their stress and moods. They can then concentrate on helping the other (previously "unfair") person to understand and accept how behaving differently would be in his or her best interest. For example, a wife whose husband does (she believes) too little of the housework can then work (confront and track positives) constructively to help her husband accept that it would be in his better interest to help out more.

Still, all this seems pessimistic. I mean, there's such a thing as the right thing to do or the moral thing to do, and I was raised to believe that people *ought to* do what's right. I try to do the correct thing. I treat people the way they deserve even when it doesn't suit me to do it. What it comes down to, I guess, is that I treat other people fairly. So don't I have the right to think they *should* do the same for me?

The *should* and *ought to* you're using take us back to what I said before about oughty thinking. If you go back over that section, you'll see that what you believe to be the right thing may *not* be what others believe. You don't have the only grasp on what's right and wrong in the world. Besides, if you are looking out for others that much, then they're a lot better off than you are. They have both themselves and you looking out for them. That puts you at an extreme disadvantage. You deserve better!

Remember how I described life as sometimes being like walking through a forest with a flashlight? When you get stressed about others not treating you fairly, you're the person complaining about other people not keeping their lights at your feet while you are busy shining your light at the feet of others. It's much more reasonable to keep your light at your own feet and accept the fact that others, if they're smart, will do the same.

All this seems like a lot to do and even more to learn. Why should anyone need to learn these things? It seems to me that they ought to come naturally.

Some children are able to interpret accurately what's going on around them and they have more people making sure they are exposed to the truth. As adults, eagle thinking seems to come "naturally for them." In fact it doesn't. They just learned eagle thinking earlier than the rest of us.

"Making Magic" Thinking

This faulty way of thinking may well cause more needless stress, heartache, and poor moods than any other. It is what most of us call "worry."

What do you mean by worry?

My definition? Dwelling on something you consider "bad" that has happened or might happen. Once you're thinking about it, it's difficult to get your mind off it even when you'd like not to think about it.

As children, we see grownups doing something they call "worrying." Since they're grownups and therefore smarter than we are, we figure there must be some value in worry (it sure isn't obvious to us). We do know that little of what's worried about ever actually happens, or isn't that bad if it does happen. Also, the people we see worrying are typically those we identify as loving us. Ah so! We finally understand.

The "value" of worrying is that it magically (kids believe in magic) keeps bad stuff from happening or keeps it from being that bad, if it does happen. Also, it's a demonstration of love—it magically conveys love to the person worried about. (I've noticed over the years that many people who worry in an attempt to convey love to others were rarely told they were loved as children.) Sure enough—when we worry, we find that (like magic) most of what we worry about never happens, and if it does happen it isn't nearly so bad as we imagined (worried) it might be. We notice that people we worry about love us and we think (mistakenly and unknowingly) that it must have been our worry that let them know we loved them too.

By the time we get to be adults, we've already learned to do the magic thinking called "worry" and have got addicted to it. That's right, addicted. Worry is like a drug we feel compelled to use even when our good sense knows it does no real good, never has and never will, and serves only to create stress and make our lives and moods miserable at times.

It amazes me how often we feel somehow superior to heroin addicts or alcohol addicts. If we worry, we're as "hooked" as they are. Our drug (worry) may be more socially acceptable and not as obviously hurtful, but it's no less an addiction! And it may not be any less harmful than other addictions.

Part of the tragedy of worrying is that when we worry about those we love, especially children, we subtly give the message that worry is love. "If you love somebody, you worry about them." If children accept that as reality, we're passing along much needless grief. They'll later worry about those they love. Still worse, their ability to express love more openly, to more openly say, "I love you," will be lessened.

Are you saying that I'm not only needlessly hurting myself with worry, but I'm actually hurting people I love by worrying about them?

No, because it isn't possible to make someone accept worrying as a good thing when it absolutely isn't. If you give that message (worry is good) through your behavior, and your children accept it as valid, then that's ultimately their responsibility but you were not a positive influence. A part of your responsibility to your children is to be a positive influence—to figure out and tell them what is the truth.

Still another problem with worry is that it subtly but seriously hinders self-acceptance and self-love by violating the Be of Be in the here and now. When we are worrying, we're totally out of the here and now and are (in our imagination) in the past or in the future. When we are worrying we're shining our light anywhere but at our feet. The prospect of stumbling is far greater.

"Can't" Thinking

When we say "can't" we're most often saying something that's entirely untrue. "Can't" means we're physically or mentally unable to do something.

As children, we were told "you can't" mostly because grownups didn't want us to know the truth—that we did have an option. If we'd known we had a choice, we might have gone against their wishes and, they would have thought, made life more difficult for them. Occasionally, we see through the untruth of "you can't" (you have no option) and rebel: "Yes, I can."

But because as children we readily believed what we were told by grownups, we accepted and even began to tell ourselves things that weren't true. "I *can't* make good grades." "I *can't* be as popular as Sally." "I just *can't* help it." "I *can't* remember to take out the trash."

Taking the word "can't" into adult life, it's even more often a lie. As adults we're far more physically and mentally able to act than we were as children. If "can't" was untrue 85 percent of the time we used it as a child, it is untrue 99 percent of the time when we use it as adults.

We pay a dear price in secret self-esteem each time we say "I can't." Our subconscious takes the words "I can't" very literally: there is no choice. Since our subconscious mind knows that others have choices and are capable of doing what we say we "can't," it takes that to mean that we are inferior to others, we aren't as capable mentally or physically as others. That most definitely lowers our self-esteem.

Most people say, "I can't," at least sometimes. Even people I know who have good self-esteem say it.

The greater a person's sense of self-worth—especially the secret kind—the less often it's expressed. Even those of us with better self-esteem pay a price. The more it's avoided, the better.

"I can't" violates not only the Be's of truth and awareness, it also goes against the Be of Be self-responsible. When we say "I can't" we are saying (in effect), "I'm not responsible." "I can't" is irresponsible.

When we say, for example, "I *can't* hurt someone's feelings by refusing to eat their food even if the food will make me fat," we are blaming food and other people for being fat. We are implying, whether or not we will admit it or be aware of it, that others and food control us. The truth is that because we are responsible for our fat we can correct beliefs or attitudes that get in our way. Since we are responsible, we can do something about it.

Self-control is Self-responsibility.

When we have the opposite attitude we'll think or say things such as, "It is better that someone else's feelings be hurt for a few minutes than for me to be hurt for years. I'm stronger than food—any food. I deserve good attention more than the food or drink deserves it."

So far, you've said that I am better off to avoid saying have to (gotta), can't, should, makes me feel, and it's not fair. Aren't you just playing word games?

The words aren't so important but understanding them is vital. They (and others I'll talk about later) imply a lack of essential awareness, responsibility, and belief. By being aware of your and others' use of such words, you are making a strong move toward stress mastery and all the benefits that go with it.

"I Just Know" Thinking

There's a good deal of overlap between "I just know" thinking and "making magic" thinking. When we're worrying (being a magician), often we are saying (in effect), "I just know some bad thing is going to happen" (being a fortune teller).

I tell people who are doing "I just know" thinking that, in order to do that and make money too, they need to have a sign in their front yard, with the words "Reader, Adviser, Seer" alongside a big, red hand. That would help to advertise that they can tell the future *and* read minds.

Of course none of us can truly read minds or tell the future. We may be good at guessing, but guessing is not knowing. We don't know for sure what other people will do or think until they do it or tell us.

But we go along, making comments such as, "I just know it's going to rain." "She doesn't like me—I just know she doesn't." "I know the economy is going to get worse." "I'll bet he's going to say 'no' when I ask him to buy." "He thinks I'm ugly." "If I ask her for a date, she's going to laugh at me." And so on.

"I just know" thinking is a favorite of people who experience dangerous levels of stress that lead to needless fear, panic, tension, anxiety, or nervousness. They often forecast the future. "I know the elevator will get stuck if I get on it." "The plane will crash." "The doors will close and I won't be able to get out." "I'll get lost if I go." "The dog will bite me." "I just know I'll step on a snake if I go in the woods." "I'll make a fool of myself if I give a speech." Unfortunately, the endless possibilities for such talk are quite limiting.

I am afraid to speak in front of groups, but I don't think I tell myself something bad is going to happen. It just scares me.

Remember what I said before about subconscious or automatic thinking? There are thoughts going on in our brain and we don't even realize it. If you are afraid to speak in front of a group (or afraid of anything else), then you are scaring yourself with fortune telling. ("I just know I'll forget what I want to say and make a complete fool of myself.")

As with "making magic" thinking, "I just know" thinking violates the Be's of Be truthful and Be in the here and now. One of the great benefits of living in the here and now, of forcing ourselves to pay attention to what's going on at this moment, is that there is very little to be afraid of in the present. Most fear is based in thoughts of some imagined future that probably won't happen anyway.

There is little to be frightened of in the present. Most fear is involved with the future.

You're saying that if I keep my mind focused on what's going on now instead of knowingly or unknowingly dwelling on the future, which I don't know anyway, then I won't be afraid. That's easy to say. It's another thing to be able to do it.

You can do it. You are worth whatever it takes to do it. The best time to practice (and it does take practice) focusing on the present time is when you aren't afraid or nervous. Every once in a while, concentrate on what's happening around you right then. Be aware of your sensations. Do you feel a breeze? What do you hear near you that you haven't noticed before? Look at each object in the room you're in. Pay close attention to each detail.

By practicing that concentration regularly when you aren't afraid or are less fearful, you'll find it easier to do when you're scaring yourself with "I just know" thinking.

Before we go on, let me give a personal example of "I just know" thinking. I used to feel more and more scared, the closer I got to my office. I'd notice some signs of stress such as a funny feeling in my stomach. I'd tell myself, "This is silly. Why am I doing this?" Then I came to understand that without realizing it I was thinking something such as, "I just know that when I get to the office some kind of crisis will be going on." I was shining my flashlight way ahead on my path. Regardless of whether a crisis was waiting, it was doing no good to anticipate (expect) it. I began to practice paying attention to what I was passing, along the highway. I felt comfortable and got to my office calm and better able to deal with what was happening.

How come you would be thinking (and not know it) that something bad was going to be happening at your office? Did it happen that there was usually some crisis there?

A colleague once told me, "There really is a difference between laboratory rats and human beings. Rats learn better. You reward a rat for going through a maze, and it will go on just as long as it gets the reward. Stop rewarding it, with food or whatever, and it just won't go on anymore. But if you reward a human only once for going through a maze, he might keep on going the rest of his life, without rewards."

Humans are far better than rats at imagining. If we get reinforced just once, we can imagine the reward afterward, even when we're not getting it. I suspect that's a big reason why people keep dieting. They hardly ever get rewarded, but they imagine they will.

Anyway, maybe once, years before, I got to my office to find a disturbance of some sort was going on. My imagination took over after that, and I didn't even know I was imagining. My subconscious mind was trying to do me a favor by preparing me for a crisis that didn't happen. The misguided purpose of "I just know" thinking is to prepare us for happenings that we mistakenly believe upset us ("makes me feel" thinking). It's much the same as tensing your arm in preparation for a blood test. Tensing up just makes the needle stick more uncomfortable.

"Grate Expectations" Thinking

With "grate expectations" thinking, we're having expectations that grate on (wear down) our self-esteem and relationships, aren't realistic, and are likely to be perfectionistic.

Expecting that others, and life, will treat us fairly is an example of a "grate" expectation. Expecting that others will be like us—work as quickly, be as conscientious, be as honest, be as thoughtful— is another example of "grate expectations." Other people aren't us; they're themselves, with different experiences, interests, goals, knowledge, desires, and concerns.

It's also a "grate expectation" when we expect someone to be someone else. We might, for example, expect our husband or wife to be like our father or mother. We may expect our lover to be like a movie star or some ideal man or woman we've created in our mind. We might expect one of our children to be like another of our children or like an adult. These are only some of the many unrealistic expectations that create needless stress for us and hurt our relationships.

When we expect others to be as we are or as others are, we are denying the truth of their difference from us and others. We are unaware of the value of their difference; we are aware only of the difference in their behavior, and we find their behavior unacceptable.

Do you mean that if someone is doing something I don't like, it's wrong for me to do anything about it?

On the contrary. You have a very definite responsibility to do what you can if someone's behavior directly and negatively affects you. But what you do needs to be based on truthful awareness of what's going on. Let me explain.

When someone is doing something you don't like, that person can affect you on one of two counts: (1) interfering with fulfillment of one or more of your needs, and (2) going against your values (what you believe is right and wrong).

How do you decide which is which; which is needs and which is values?

Well, needs are essentials, such as having enough food and water, being safe, enjoying ourselves. Values have to do with what we think is good or not good to do. Most of us have the value that stealing is wrong.

I'll give you an example that can be either need or value. Let's say you don't smoke and people near you are smoking. If you're breathing their smoke and are having difficulty breathing, then their smoking is interfering with your meeting the need to breathe comfortably and maintain good health. If you're not breathing their smoke but you believe that people are better off to avoid smoking because it hurts them, then their smoking is going against your values.

Take another example from a work situation. If someone you work with isn't doing his or her assigned work and you end up doing it, that person's behavior is violating your needs. You may need to spend more time on your own work, to not be rushed, or to not work overtime. But if the only effect of someone's not doing assigned work is that you don't like it, you have a values disagreement.

If you don't like what another person is doing you can do one of three things:

1. You can determine that you have a "grate expectation" and are unrealistically expecting too much. In that case you say nothing.

2. If your expectation is not unrealistic and if others' behavior violates a need of yours, you can constructively confront. (I'll explain constructive confrontation shortly.)

3. If there's a values difference, you can offer to share your values with others with the understanding that if they aren't interested, you'll back off. For instance, if they are smoking and you're concerned about their health, you might say something like, "I know some things I'd like to tell you about smoking and how it affects people. Is that all right with you?" If they say "yes," go to it. If they say they aren't interested, then you need to leave them alone. You might offer again later, but for right then, drop it.

Constructive Confrontation

Constructive confrontation, with the emphasis on *constructive,* is among the most important skills a stress master has. And it is a learned skill. No one is born knowing how to do it. The essential elements of constructive confrontation are:

- You make a brief, clear, and non-critical statement of what the other person has or hasn't done and how one of your needs is not being met, or might not be met in the future, as a consequence.
- If there's a negative or questioning reaction to your statement of need, let the person confronted know you heard and understood the reaction. (Understanding doesn't mean you agree with it, of course.) You may also need to clarify something about your opening statement.
- When the person being confronted has not yet agreed to a change of behavior and you still need to confront, reword and restate your unmet need.
- You continue until there's some resolution. Some form of compromise may be involved.

Too often we think of confrontation as being aggressive, angry, critical, an effort to win at the other's expense, and hit-and-run. In fact, effective confrontation is none of these. An example will help to clarify.

Statement of Behavior and Need. "Sally, I haven't received the report I asked for last week. To make sure our clients get what they want on time and to keep me from getting fussed at by my supervisor,

it will now be necessary for me to work late. And I need my time off."
(The need in this case is adequate time off from work. Another possible need might be avoiding getting in trouble with the supervisor. The statement was clear and not attacking. One good way to avoid attacking or being critical is to avoid, as much as you can, using the word "you" in the statement of need.)

Negative or Questioning Response. Sally says, "But I didn't know you wanted the report any time soon. You always do this to me. You tell me to do something and don't tell me when you need it. Besides, I've got so much to do right now. You know this is the busiest time of the year."

Your Response. To let her know you have heard her you might say something such as the following. You start by rewording some of what she said. "You didn't know when the report was due and it seems to you that I never tell you when reports are due. And you're right—this is the busy time of the year." Then you restate your need using somewhat different words. "I'll do what I can to give you more lead time on future projects. But for right now we need to take care of this one. I'm concerned that to get the report completed on time, it will be necessary for me to give up some of my time off from work."

Since your interest is to get your need met, rather than argue with Sally, you have let her know that you understood what she said without agreeing or disagreeing. Then you have restated your need not to miss time off from work. You are prepared to do this until you get an agreeable settlement of the issue.

Possible Continued Response from Person Confronted. "Okay, I understand you need your time off. What do you want me to do about it?" Sally may now be ready for you to suggest a solution such as that she stop what she is doing and get the report done or perhaps put in some overtime herself. If she disagrees, you can ask her to suggest how the report can get done *and* you get your time off from work. If resolution is still bogged down, go back to restating the gist of what you understand she is telling you and restate your statement of behavior and need.

I'm not sure this would work, and besides, it sounds funny. It doesn't sound like something I'd say to somebody.

The best way to be sure it does work is to test it out more than once. I hope you'll do that. If it doesn't sound like you, maybe it's because

you avoid confronting or when you do confront you don't do it constructively. Only you can know that for sure.

Try this exercise, to get good at constructive confrontation.
Think back to a situation where someone was acting or not acting in
a way that interfered with the meeting of your needs. Perhaps someone got ahead of you in line and interfered with your need to get
through the line quickly. Maybe lukewarm food was brought to you,
and you need that particular food to be served hot. Then write out
the parts of the confrontation you might have done.

What most often stops people from confronting is fear—
often, fear of anger ("She might get upset." "I might irritate
him if I tell him this."). The fear of anger comes from a basic
misunderstanding; the truth is, *anger comes from fear.*

You see, stress leads to what I call the "Hike, Hit, or Hide
Consequence." Human BE-ings, who do not yet have the skill
to do otherwise, generate uncomfortable emotions needed to
fuel the actions that will hopefully overcome whatever (real
or imagined) is seen as a threat. The "Hike" emotion is the
fear that enables someone to run away or escape. The "Hit"
emotion is *anger* and helps a person to verbally or nonverbally
strike out against the threat. The "Hide" emotion is *depression*
and is intended to help avoid danger by laying low. The first
response to what is thought to be a threat is fear. Then there is
a mental evaluation of the situation that is extremely fast and
subconscious. As a result of that evaluation, the fear remains
fear, or takes the form of either anger or depression—"hit" or
"hide."

Once we have understood that anger is based on fear, we're
less likely to be afraid of (or reluctant to confront) someone who
is, in fact, fearful. The other person is showing his or her fear
through anger. Also, we are less likely to become angry with
someone who's showing this fear.

Back to Expectations

Again, "grate expectations" thinking is duck-like thinking that involves expecting other people, society, life, government, or anything

else to be ideal or perfect (or nearly so) in actions toward us and others. It means expecting more than is realistic. Expecting to be treated fairly is an example of "grate expectations" thinking.

Further, when people act toward us in ways we don't like, we're able to respond most truthfully when we first decide what the situation is. Is it a situation that involves having (or potentially having) trouble meeting our needs, or is it a situation that involves differences in values? (The example I gave before involved someone else's smoking.) Then we can decide if our expectation is a "grate" one, needlessly grating on our level of stress, emotions, and relationships. If it is a "grate expectation," then we need to be aware of that, accept it, and do nothing but work on ourselves.

On the other hand, if our expectation isn't believed to be a "grate expectation," we can confront constructively, using the methods and responses we have just discussed.

So far, I've talked about grate expectations where others are concerned. We can also have grate expectations of ourselves, expecting more of ourselves than is reasonable. I've sometimes called this "self-comparison" thinking, when we compare ourselves to someone else or some ideal self and judge ourselves as flunking the comparison.

It's important to understand that the only person we can reasonably compare ourselves to, or expect to be "as good as," is ourselves as we are right now. We are perfectly *us;* comparisons don't make good sense. Why compare perfect with perfect? Remember, behavior and physical appearance are only add-ons to what's truly and uniquely us.

Tracking Positives

"Tracking positives" is a powerful way to influence others when confrontation isn't called for or as an alternate. It absolutely eliminates the need for harsh criticism and fosters the best of positive relationships. And it's so simple.

To track positives of other people, let the other person know when he or she is doing something you like, then follow that with a nonjudgmental statement about how you would like for him or her to behave in the future.

For example, let's say your spouse takes food and drinks to the den and leaves the dirty dishes there. You want him or her to take the dishes back to the kitchen and put them in the sink. First, you need to determine something that's positive about what your spouse is already doing and how to express what it is you would like. You might then say, "You are careful not to spill things when you eat and drink in the den, and I appreciate that. I would also appreciate it if you would take the dishes back to the kitchen and put them in the sink." A judgmental (wrong) way of saying the preceding might be: "I wish you would be less *lazy* in the future and take your dishes back to the kitchen." Avoid negative judgments.

Tracking positives is extremely effective in influencing others. It also works great on ourselves because it avoids self-criticism, has reliable results, and doesn't damage our surface or secret self-esteem.

How can I use tracking positives on myself?

Here's a personal example. As a writer, I definitely want to encourage (influence) myself to write. One way I do that is to occasionally read something I wrote at least a year before. When I note improvements I would make, which doesn't take long at all, I compliment myself. I track my positive by telling myself, "I sure have improved in my skill as a writer to be able to recognize so many spots that need changes. That's terrific!"

Wrapping It Up

Now we've reviewed some of the more common and damaging ways of thinking and talking. In addition, we've talked about two ways to influence others, to get our important needs met. Those ways were constructive confrontation and tracking positives.

A few of the major points made in this chapter were:

- What you and I believe to be true ultimately determines our moods and level of stress.
- Saying and thinking we "can't" or we "gotta" are useless remnants of childhood that deny the reality of the choices we have, promote damaged self-esteem, and avoid essential responsibility.
- There's no "fair" in the world, except where you find ferris wheels. And righteous indignation is not an effective way to encourage needed change.

- When we, as adults, maintain the childhood illusion that we can somehow tell the future and read the minds of others, we pay a great and needless price in fear and anger. We hurt our relationships and act contrary to reality.

- By expecting more of ourselves and others than is reasonable, we deny the perfection we all share. Our actions, feelings, and physical attributes are not perfect, because they are not us. What is truly us deserves our respect and unconditional love. How can we reasonably expect ourselves and others to be better than perfect?

"Remember, the duck stops here."

6

More Quacked Quotes

Additional Ways of Thinking That
Create Hurtful Stress in You

Whenever you are experiencing excess stress you'll probably recognize your thoughts as one of the defective ways of thinking described in Chapter 5. Still other problem ways of thinking that I've identified over the years deserve attention. Here are some more "quacked quotes."

Faulty Thinking: Placing Blame

Some time ago, a woman brought into a therapy session a list of acts she thought her husband had done to hurt her and their marriage. Later, I was talking to my wife Judy, a registered nurse, who has been trained as a co-therapist. (She sometimes serves as my case consultant, although the identity of the client isn't revealed.) I told her, "A woman brought in a list of acts her husband had done that she said had ruined their marriage. She said these actions hurt her very badly. Thinking back, I realize I've talked with other men who've done much worse than this husband. And what they have done hasn't hurt their marriage all that much. I wonder what the difference is."

Judy said, "Perhaps their wives didn't keep score."

Couples in marriage counseling often say, "But he [she] lied to me."

Most often it turns out that one is lying no more than the other, but one of them is telling more socially acceptable untruths.

To me, what Judy was saying was that those other wives didn't spend much time placing fault or blame—what I call faulty thinking. They weren't making nearly so much needless stress for themselves.

Guilt is a feeling many parent-like people encourage in us as children, as a way of trying to control or manipulate our behavior. Placing blame or fault encourages guilt. "It's all your fault. You didn't do what you were supposed to do and things went wrong." Fairly soon, as children, we learn to place fault—to do faulty thinking—ourselves. "I didn't do it. Johnny did it." We hope to avoid punishment and feelings of guilt. Ultimately, we hope to protect our self-esteem.

Placing fault or blame is all tied to the mistaken belief that people are what they do. "Good people do only good things and bad people do bad things." If somehow we can prove other people are at fault or at least more at fault than we are, we think (consciously or subconsciously) that will mean we are a better people and safer than they are. We are more deserving of kindness, respect, love, and attention.

Increasingly, I suspect there are actually only two emotions: *love* and *fear.* Other "feelings" are simply expressions of those emotions. Joy is love felt intensely. Anger is fear turned outward. Depression is fear (in the form of anger) turned on ourselves. Jealousy is fear of loss, and so on.

As adults, we need to move away from the faulty thinking of childhood because (1) it encourages needless stress, conflict, hurt, and anger, and (2) it is looking for the problem rather than for the solution. Faulty thinking seeks to avoid responsibility. And being self-responsible is essential to self-acceptance and self-love at the secret level.

"Don't Like" Thinking

"Don't you like Sally?" "Do you like hamburgers or pizzas best?" "You like your teacher, don't you?" As children, we often hear statements and questions that imply that what we like or don't like is very important. As adults we then believe that being around people or things we don't like is a major problem. We make comments such as, "I don't *like* this part of my job." "I just don't *like* my job at all." "I don't *like* vegetables that much." "I never did *like* school all that well." "I don't *like* Ted."

My point is this: *From the start, it was untrue that what we liked or didn't like was all that important.*

Wait. What do you mean, what I like or don't like isn't all that important? I think it's important. I try to do as many of the things I like as I possibly can and I try to avoid as many of the things I don't like as I can.

I don't mean what you like is totally unimportant. It just isn't all-important and certainly isn't most important.

What is more important than what I like?

I'm glad you asked. *What likes you is far more important than what you like.* (I'm defining "liking" as wanting to be helpful to you, wanting to help you succeed, being protective and not hurtful.)

Let me give an example. A while back, my physician was concerned I might have a problem with my heart. To learn more, he asked me to wear a heart monitor for a 24-hour period. The monitor itself weighed several pounds and the electrodes were glued and taped to my chest. It was heavy and in the way, and sleeping with it was no fun at all. After maybe 15 or 16 hours of wearing this gadget I was upset. Aware that I was upset, I asked myself what I might be thinking. Readily the answer I came up with was, "I *don't like* this monitor!"

What I then told myself was, "The fact is that this monitor likes me. It'll help keep me safe. It might even save my life." It definitely liked me and whether I liked it (the monitor) was beside the point. I immediately felt much better.

Some friends who've learned to be eagle thinkers told me that their nine-year-old son suddenly began refusing to do his homework. When asked why, he simply said, "I don't like it." After gently encouraging him to tell them more, they carefully explained that they understood. Neither of them had particularly liked homework when they were in school, but homework had definitely liked them and it liked him too. They explained that doing his homework and doing well in school would help him to get a job and make a good living. Yes, school and homework were just crazy about him.

Later that evening, the parents noticed that he was dutifully doing his homework. His father said, "I thought you didn't care for homework." The boy said, "I still don't, but it likes me."

Who and what we like often reflects how well we like ourselves. A teenage girl once told me, "The boys I like don't seem to like me or they don't like me for long. The boys who think a lot of me don't interest me." The reason for this turned out to be that the boys she was most likely to care for weren't young men who were apt to be nice to her for very long. They were interested in themselves, not in commitment. Because she didn't like herself, she found it difficult to trust anyone who liked her. How could she trust anyone so dumb as to like her?

Many other words can be used as substitutes for *like*—such words as "prefer," "want," or "love." When you hear yourself using such words, ask yourself, "But does he [or she or it] like me? If not, what does that imply about how I feel about myself?"

"What People Say Matters Most" Thinking

I recall reading a story about a wise teacher and his student. The student was fond of occasionally making comments to the teacher that he believed would have irritated or even infuriated most people, but didn't seem to bother the teacher.

One day the student said something to the teacher that he knew would have made most people extremely angry and, as usual, the teacher paid no attention. Frustrated, the student asked, "How come you don't get angry at what I say?" The teacher thought a moment and said, "Oh yeah, I used to get upset over what people said. That was back when I thought what people said was most important."

At first, what I thought about that idea bothered me. Then I finally understood what the teacher most likely meant: What people *mean* matters much more than what people actually say.

I strongly encourage you to assume that if someone says something to you and you are upset, you don't yet understand what they mean.

Over the years I've learned that, when I better understand what people mean by what they say, I'm not upset. It amazed me to find that out. The better you and I understand, the less likely we are to be stressed and upset.

If people make fun of or disapprove of you, they are expressing their own insecurities. By trying to bring you down, they hope to raise themselves up and repair their damaged self-esteem.

If you respond to such criticism with hurt, fear, or anger (fear with a mean face) it means you're unsure your actions are correct. You need to examine what you are doing, in order to determine the truth.

As you become more advanced in stress mastery, you may find it a great advantage to regularly associate with someone who is often critical of you. This gives you a regular opportunity to get straight about what you do and don't believe and to determine just how committed you are to what you believe.

The first version of something that is written is very rarely what gets published. Anything in print has probably been rewritten once or twice and then edited at least a couple of times.

So what's the point?

Much the same holds true for what you say. If you're a good communicator and an eagle thinker, the first time you say something is going in the direction of what you actually mean, but most likely isn't there yet. To be most truly what you mean, what you said at first would need to be thought about and changed at least once, if not two or three times.

Yet, we tend to take what we and others say the first time as exactly what's meant. And it isn't. You're wise to assume that what you and others say is only the "first draft." To get at what's truly meant, when that's important to do, will need more thought and redoing.

"Get Even" Thinking

Occasionally when I am working with a group in a seminar there will be someone who, for some reason, is hard to get along with. He or she talks to other group participants while I'm talking, asks me challenging questions, and makes negative statements. I'm still tempted (very briefly) to get even with such people, but when I realized (became aware of) the truth, the urge to "get even" with them pretty much left me.

I came to understand there was nothing I could do to such people that would have been nearly so hurtful as what they would do to themselves. For one thing, they were avoiding the many benefits I offered to the group—benefits others were getting. I also realized that getting even is only appropriate in wars and in games. Unless we want to play at life rather than live it or want to be at war with others, we are exceedingly smart if we avoid trying to get even.

Get smart, not even! Getting smart means using accurate thinking. When you think the truth, there's no need to try to get even.

"Always/Never" Thinking

What I term "always/never" thinking means thinking and talking in absolutes. Examples of this would be, "You *always* try to tell me what to do." "You *never* compliment me." "*Every time* I call you, you just complain." "You are *always* late." "You are *just like* your mother." "*All* the people there said . . . ."

To begin with, absolutes such as "always, never, just like, and every time" are very likely to be untrue. Rarely are things altogether one way or the other.

When you speak in absolutes, they are usually so obviously untrue that whoever hears what you say immediately trusts you less. When you talk to yourself using such absolute words, your subconscious mind trusts you less, which hurts your subconscious (secret) self-esteem.

Using absolutes often shows a significant lack of important awareness. Whoever uses them is unaware they are often untrue.

I don't see the harm in occasionally saying *always* or *never* even if technically they aren't true. What harm can it do?

Doing it once does the same harm as smoking a single cigarette; it doesn't make that much difference. The problem is that the effects pile up and those accumulated effects do damage by raising your stress and hurting your secret self-esteem. I hope you'll avoid absolutes. With awareness, avoiding them is easy, and you're definitely worth the benefits.

"If Only" Thinking

When we make comments such as, "*If only* I didn't have to ("mind in the gotta" thinking) work so hard, I could . . . ," we are in a sense making a wish. We could just as easily say, "I *wish* I didn't have to work so hard so I could . . . ."

As children, we are taught that wishing works, that wishing on a star makes dreams come true, no matter who you are. What I say is, "A good wish and a dollar bill will get you a dollar's worth of anything you want." Wishing is useless.

A wish ("if only") is a child's answer to a problem. It is based on an untruth, a lack of awareness, and an avoiding of responsibility. As with worrying, it only *seems* to help. The damage it actually does is considerable and long-lasting.

Adults and stress masters of any age solve problems by finding out the facts (truth), being aware of options, taking responsibility, and staying in the present (tackling a problem one thoughtful step at a time).

"I Can Make Up For" Thinking

Many problems, including high levels of damaging stress, experienced by people come from this subconscious and false thought. Men and women are sometimes irresistibly drawn to and marry alcoholics (sometimes even before they begin drinking) because (unknown to them) they hope to somehow "make up for" the love they didn't get from an alcoholic or drug-dependent parent. Some people abuse alcohol and other drugs with the hidden thought that the "fun" they get will help make up for the suffering of earlier times. Eating expensive or fattening food will make up for the times when food was not plentiful or was cheap. The examples are endless.

The truth is we cannot make up for what we missed out on or believe we were denied before. When we try, we make matters worse. Being married to an alcoholic is no better and may even be worse than being the child of one. Being addicted to alcohol or some other drug is certainly not a positive replacement for a troubled youth. Being fat and in poor physical condition is not a sane way of making up for previous deprivation.

Perhaps the false idea that we can make up for what we missed out on before came from childhood, when we could make up for tests missed in school. But life is not school and we are not children.

Thinking we can somehow make up for what was missed is shining our flashlight on the path behind us rather than at our feet. No wonder we then stumble and get hurt. "I can make up for" is big-time duck thinking and you and I are not ducks.

I've often been told, "But my mom [or dad or whoever] didn't love me. No wonder I'm so messed up [faulty thinking]. If only [wishy thinking] I could somehow *make up for* the love they didn't give me or if only I could get them to love me now, life would be so much better for me."

I then ask, "Do you believe that your mom [or whoever] did much eagle thinking when you were growing up or is doing much of it now?"

"No, she was quite a duck thinker then and she still is. I guess you could say I was raised in a flock of ducks."

Then I give a reminder that being consistently "loved" (the conditional kind) or approved of by a duck thinker would have been no compliment at all. What would have been required to be "loved" (or is required now to be "loved") would only make life miserable. The requirement is to be a duck thinker too.

"I'm My Shirt" Thinking

As I said earlier, what we truly are, what we were born with, is perfect. Everything else has been added on since we got here. In the same way, your shirt is not part of you. It has been added. What you do or think or even feel is no more a part of what's truly you than your shirt or shoes.

When we think or do or feel what we don't like and want to change, we mistakenly believe we are unacceptable, not worthwhile somehow. We subconsciously think, "I think bad thoughts, so I'm a bad person. I'm angry, so I am an angry [bad] person. I do bad things, so I am bad."

Are you saying it doesn't matter what I do or think or feel, because it isn't really me? I don't need to change it?

Not any more than I would suggest you not change your shirt when it begins to smell. It's a good idea to change what you need to change. Just don't confuse what you're changing with yourself. You are still worthwhile, of great value, and entirely acceptable, even if some of what you do, feel, or think isn't.

Hindsight-Labels Thinking

With this thinking, we examine our past actions or lack of action and judge ourselves negatively, giving ourselves some negative label such as "bad" or "stupid." We get after ourselves for not doing better in the past and create considerable excess stress. We mistakenly think that what we did in the past said something about our value. Again we are shining our flashlight behind us on the path rather than keeping it near our feet, where it needs to be. We very much need to be and stay in the here and now.

We can definitely learn from the past, but we don't change it! Getting after ourselves or punishing ourselves only damages the self-esteem we need to treat ourselves and others as well as we and others truly deserve.

Any misbehavior comes out of feeling badly about ourselves and others. Punishing ourselves only results in our feeling worse. We just maintain the cycle!

When we can look back and recognize what we did that didn't work out, we have grown. We need to accentuate that awareness of growth, a positive rather than a negative.

It is important to avoid placing negative labels on the behavior of ourselves and others. Giving ourselves and others negative labels like "stupid" or "foolish" just makes stress worse.

"Terrible" Thinking

"Terrible" thinking is when we put strong, negative labels on what is happening or has happened. "This is *terrible.*" "This is just the *worst* thing that has ever happened to me." "What a *horrible* situation this is." "I can't believe this *nightmare* is happening."

I can make my point best by telling a story—my adaptation of an ancient oriental parable. About 120 years ago, there was a farm family in the Western part of our country. The family consisted of a middle-aged man, his married son, daughter-in-law, and small grandchild. They had many acres of land, but no cattle and only one broken-down stallion used for plowing and pulling a wagon. They were poor and barely surviving.

One day their horse ran off. "This is *terrible,*" they said. "We are going to starve" ("I just know" thinking). They were very stressed, frightened, and exceedingly depressed. A few days later, their horse returned and brought a herd of wild mares and colts with him.

The family said, "This is wonderful. The horse running away was the best thing that ever happened. Now we can break and sell horses to the cavalry and have money to buy cattle and plant-seed."

While the married son was breaking one of the mares, he was thrown and broke his arm. The family thought, "What a *horrible* thing to happen. This is so *bad.* How can grandpa handle all the heavy chores by himself?"

The next day, the calvary came, because a group of Indians was off the reservation and making trouble. The cavalry wanted to draft the father or his son to help get the Indians back onto the reservation. It would be highly dangerous work.

The family was pleased, because neither the son nor the father could go. They thought that the son's breaking his arm was a lucky thing to happen after all. Then the troopers took some of the horses that had been broken, and paid in government script. This too was a wonderful thing. The family would, for many years, remember the day their horse ran off as the luckiest day in their lives.

The point is: the only happenings in life that are truly terrible, horrible, bad, or tragic are those that have no good outcome. It very rarely, if ever, happens that there isn't some good outcome to events in our lives that seemed negative at first.

I can see how things that happen can seem bad at first and then turn out all right or even real good. And how it's useless to be all stressed out over them in the first place. But I think it's probably human nature to react this way.

I frequently hear comments such as, "I guess it's just the way I am." "I must have been born that way." "That's just her way." "It's only natural for people to react that way." These people are talking about some action seen as hurtful and are excusing it. By calling the action "natural" or whatever, they are saying it's beyond changing.

There is absolutely nothing in my experience so far that encourages me to believe that damaging stress, bad moods, or misbehavior are natural and beyond altering. In fact, just the opposite is true.

"Yes, But" Thinking

The last comment you made is an example of still another way of thinking that creates stress. I call it "Yes, but" thinking.

Professionals who counsel people with problems hear "Yes, but" a lot. The person saying "Yes, but" is unknowingly (or knowingly) refusing to face something that's true or that he or she believes is true. "But" ("however, still," etc.) cancels agreement with what has been said.

Let me give an example. I told a client I believed her negative reaction to using affirmations (short, positive statements made to oneself) to relieve stress and feel better was based on her feeling so badly about herself. (We had previously agreed she had a very poor opinion of herself.) I went on to tell her that by realizing the truth and using affirmations anyway, she would make a big step toward loving herself.

Her response was, *"All right* [yes], I can see that it would maybe help if I could just get myself to change the way I think about myself. *But* I just can't ["can't" thinking] seem to get myself to do it."

This woman's "Yes, but" really meant the statement that followed the "All right" was untrue. She still had not accepted (Be-lieve) that her thinking about herself was faulty. She was still refusing to face the truth about her duck-like thinking.

Whenever you hear yourself saying "Yes, but," regardless of the particular words you use to say it, a bell needs to go off in your head alerting you to the possible falsehood you're telling yourself. While you are saying, "Yes, I agree with you, but . . ." (whatever), it is highly likely that you don't really believe what you are saying. You are kidding yourself and holding on to a problem and to dangerous stress.

"Don't" Thinking

Saying "I don't think" often means you're mistakenly and subconsciously trying to "protect" or build your self-concept. At a deep level, you think that accepting some piece of information would threaten your secret self-esteem. Another possibility is that "I don't think" is a mistaken attempt to build your surface self-esteem by refusing to accept information. A result is that you create unnecessary stress for yourself.

That's a pretty complicated concept. Some examples would help.

I suspect that the great majority of "don't" thinking happens when you're obviously (or subtly) asking for advice or trying to analyze something you identify as a problem. When that advice or analysis is offered, you respond, out loud or to yourself, "I don't think so."

Several years ago, a business owner I know hired a consultant to evaluate his business. The consultant did the evaluation and submitted her written report. She had seven or eight major recommendations, such as increasing certain fees and reducing some staff. The business owner's immediate response was, "I don't think that's right." More than five years later, he reviewed the consultant's report and found that he had eventually put into effect every one of her suggestions. Had he done so much earlier, he might have saved himself considerable stress and money. I suspect he didn't accept the suggestions earlier because he was attempting to protect his hurt secret self-esteem. He thought, without knowing it, the recommendations implied he was inadequate. "If I were okay [adequate], such suggestions wouldn't have been made, much less need to be implemented."

A client named Susie came to counseling, saying she needed "good advice" and some accurate interpretations of what was happening in her life. She told about her unhappy childhood and about going as an adult from one unfulfilling, romantic relationship to another. She was often sad and had many physical symptoms of severe and chronic stress.

Repeatedly, I gave the "good advice" she said she wanted. Most times, her responses were, "I don't think so." "I don't *feel* [another word that really means think] that's true." "I just don't *believe* [another word substituted for think] . . . ." After several counseling sessions, I was confused. If Susie agreed with so little of what I said, why did she keep coming for counseling and become upset when I suggested that she might want to stop?

I told her that I suspected she was being hurt by an inaccurate way of thinking called "don't" thinking, and briefly explained it. Without hesitation, she exclaimed, "*I don't think* that's right."

Susie was trying to enhance her secret self-esteem by disagreeing with someone (me) she identified as an authority. Each time she said, "I don't think . . . ," she implied to herself that she wasn't inferior, as she suspected she was. By implying that she knew more than the expert who was advising her, she was telling herself that she was adequate. She "benefited" a little at first and suffered far more in the long term. To avoid feelings of inadequacy, she was rejecting information she could have used to turn her life around in a most positive way.

Months after Susie finally dropped out of counseling, she called. She told me that she was doing well. From what she said, it was clear that she had later put into effect much of the "good advice" and insights I'd offered her before.

Does all this mean I should simply accept whatever I'm told?

Not at all. Be aware, though. When you're directly or indirectly asking for advice, watch out if you hear yourself saying (in so many words), "I don't think. . . ." The advice you're seeking could be received in person or in audio or written materials such as this book. An "I don't think" response is a red flag, a signal that you very much need to wait and think. Don't simply reject what's being told to you; it is potentially very useful. At least it's well worth your time and thought to be sure.

You are of the greatest value; you are perfectly you, and it doesn't get any better than that. If someone knows something you don't, that doesn't diminish your value at all. Since you're already entirely worthwhile, you don't enhance it by disagreeing with some expert or authority you go to for help. You decrease stress and its threat to you by accepting the truth from various sources.

"I'll Do Better When" Thinking

People who're addicted to nicotine or alcohol often adopt this thinking. Their addictive act is preceded, usually at a subconscious level, by the thought, "I'll do better later." They think, or tell themselves, they'll do something for "just a while longer." The alcoholic will drink just one more. The smoker will smoke until he or she is 30 and then stop. The problem is that these are untruths.

Thinking this way is shining our flashlight up the path; we're not living in the here and now, as we very much need to do.

Why is it essential to do "better" right now? Not because it makes us any better; we are already as "better" as anyone gets. We need to do better because we deserve far better! The temporary pleasure of the addiction isn't at all worth the price we pay.

"Poor Me" Thinking

"I can't ["can't" thinking] work like I could before. I lost my job and haven't worked for nearly two years." That was just part of what a woman told her counselor. She had been seriously injured at work and had lost partial use of her shoulder. She was absolutely sure the injury and her inability to work caused the considerable stress and severe depression she was experiencing.

Much of what she was doing was the quacked quote I have named "poor me" thinking. "Poor me, I'm not able to work like before." "Poor me, I'm not able to help support my family." She was having quite a pity party for herself.

The young woman was told about some of the athletic achievements of disabled people. She soon decided that her trouble wasn't really so bad when she thought of how hurtful it might have been. Besides, her disability wasn't her. She was not of less value because her shoulder was injured. She was not less than perfect, or less important, because she wasn't able to work.

Duck-Plays-Ostrich Thinking

Carl worried about whether a bank would hold him and his wife responsible for more than $100,000 in loans owed by his former employer. Carl had been given a good deal of responsibility by his boss, supervising other employees and even occasionally signing company checks. When the business failed and the owner–boss left town giving no forwarding address and owing all that money, the bank easily found Carl and told him that he owed the money. The bank reasoned that he must own at least some of the company, since he sometimes signed company checks.

Carl had contacted an attorney, who had promised to look into the matter and get back to him. That was months ago, and he'd not heard anything from the lawyer. He had heard from the bank, though. He had only six weeks to pay in full or go to court.

"How about calling the attorney to find out what she's learned?", Carl was asked several times over the period of weeks he was in counseling. Each time he responded with something such as, "But she said she'd call me when she knew something I needed to know."

Carl was definitely doing duck-plays-ostrich thinking. He figured that if he didn't ask, he wouldn't find out something he didn't want to know. After all, "No news is good news." The fact was that he was doing duck-like thinking and burying his head in the sand of unawareness. (He later reported that the lawyer had called his home more than once to tell him that because of a legal loophole she couldn't represent him and had done nothing at all on his case. When the attorney was unable to contact him, she finally gave up.) If he hadn't been doing duck-like thinking, he would've called the attorney and found out the status of his case much sooner, saving himself a great deal of stress.

Carl was dealing with another matter by trying not to learn and think about it. His older sister was a prescription drug addict and had recently "gone off the wagon" and back to drugs. When he reported that his sister had left treatment much too soon, it was suggested that he contact his other sisters to plan how they might act to encourage their sister to get the care she desperately needed. He refused, saying that since his other sisters lived much closer to the one with the problem, they should decide what to do. Besides, he didn't want to be the one to tell his sister she needed to go back to the hospital. Her feelings toward him might be hurt.

With both the loans and the addiction of his sister, Carl experienced much more stress by ignoring them. Knowing the facts is far better; it's part of keeping your light at your feet. You stumble much less that way.

But I've never been threatened by a bank that way and my sister isn't hooked on medicine. It's hard to see how this way of thinking applies to me.

Most of us are likely to do this kind of false thinking over what seem to be smaller matters. For example, maybe we don't balance our checkbooks often enough. "If I don't know what my balance is, then I probably have enough money to cover my checks." Then we find that bouncing checks isn't better than knowing our balance is low.

Duck-plays-ostrich thinking can be particularly deadly. Some people are doing it when they ignore signs of serious illness such as cancer or heart trouble. Please pay attention to what's happening nearby on your path. Your life and your physical and mental well-being can depend on it.

"Luck" (Sounds like Duck) Thinking

A teenager I know has gotten three tickets for speeding and even more parking citations over a period of a year and a half. He thought about it and decided he knew exactly what the problem was. "I have the worst luck. Why do all these bad things always happen to me?"

In another instance, a child and her father were talking. The girl was noting that the family had a beautiful home, many servants, and fine, expensive automobiles. Then the girl said, "Daddy, we're so lucky. Aren't we?" The dad responded, "And it's amazing how much more good luck we have, the harder I work."

"Luck" is a word used to protect us from awareness of how much hurt secret self-esteem we have. "Luck" avoids responsibility. "It's not my fault. I just had bad luck." Nearly all times the word "luck" (or sister words such as "fortunate" or "unfortunate") is used, it is absolutely untrue. We may not (probably don't) know how responsible we are for what's happened, whether we like it (good luck) or don't like it (bad luck). Still, we are responsible. We create our own luck.

A hurtful aspect of attributing what happens to luck is that we make ourselves unaware of how we act to create the stress we have. The teenager, for example, was experiencing high levels of stress. He was near losing his license or his car. Since he blamed chance (luck) rather than his driving too fast or recklessly and parking in inappropriate places, he felt helpless to protect his license.

As with the other duck-like thinking such as "can't" thinking and "makes me feel" thinking, "luck" thinking comes from and adds to hurt secret self-esteem. Recognizing that happenings we call "good" are a result of our efforts is not consistent with our low self-image. "How could a wretch like me be responsible for such wonderful happenings? It's got to be luck." By assigning happenings that we don't like to "bad luck," we avoid facing our hurt self-esteem. But facing it is the key to changing it and avoiding our stress-fueled "duck roast."

Whenever you catch yourself using "luck" or similar words, remind yourself that luck sounds like duck. It's duck-like thinking to believe in luck.

Does this mean that there aren't situations that happen by chance? I mean, if I get cancer or something, it isn't chance? I did it to myself?

The more I learn, the more I doubt there's much chance (stuff that happens over which we have no control) in the world. Without realizing we do, we influence nearly all of what happens to us, and that includes getting heart attacks and cancer. If you feel guilty about that, then you're doing another duck-like and inaccurate thinking, "I'm so bad. It's all my fault this happened to me." Remember that being truly self-responsible means focusing on the present rather than the past. Keep your light at your feet. Say to yourself, "This is happening to me and I can and will do something about it."

"It's Too Hard" Thinking

A story is told about two children going home. Their home was a wonderful place but difficult to get to. Part of the walk home involved picking their way along a mountain path. The older child was going first and holding the small hand of her brother. He was complaining with every other step. "Sister, this is hard. The rocks are sharp and hurt my feet." She turned to him, held his hand a little firmer to help reassure him, and said, "Brother, I know it's hard, but the rocks are what we climb on. If it weren't for them the path would be too slippery. We'd just slide back to the bottom. It would be a lot harder to get home than it is now."

Life is so much more difficult, and we have so much more stress, when we think it shouldn't be hard or challenging at times. The difficult acts and hard work required of us, the pain we sometimes experience, are simply parts of the path of life we need to follow to get to where we want to be. The challenging parts even serve an important purpose: somehow they insure that we don't slide back or regress.

This thing about the trouble and challenges in life helping to keep us from losing the progress we make reminds me of something a mother might say to a child, giving it medicine. "Sweetheart, I know it tastes bad. But it's so good for you."

As with the other mallard thinking, "it's too hard" thinking began in childhood. As children, we misinterpreted. We believed (incorrectly) that the less worthy we were, the harder we had to work or the more challenges we had to undertake. Without realizing it, work (doing something that isn't easy or that much fun) was seen as punishment. And why be punished? Because we were "bad." Wrong!

Observing rock musicians, movie stars, and the very wealthy, we misinterpret and inaccurately believe that the more important we are, the more we're liked and admired, and the less work or what we perceive as work we have to do. The reality is that for the vast majority of people who gain wealth, prestige, and career success, those rewards came as a result of persistence and working hard for years. To see the result of all that labor and discomfort is far easier than seeing what went into it.

How hard a person works says nothing about his or her value. Both those who don't work and those who feel badly about working so hard are only revealing something about what they believe their value is.

"Lost" Thinking

Someone I occasionally consult with called me and dejectedly announced, "Richard, I just lost $200,000." My response was, "Dave, tell me where you lost it and I'll go looking for it." He ignored my comment and went on to explain that he had not gotten two important sales, worth a gross of $200,000, because a trouble-making customer made some entirely false statements about his product to prospective buyers. Dave was stressed and angry and hoped that talking with me would provide some relief.

After listening a while, I began to explain that it wasn't the loss of the sales that was causing his upset and stress; it was his "lost" thinking. He was telling himself he had lost (was deprived of) something of real value to him. I explained that *losing something implies that you at least once had it in your possession and that you have some potential for finding it if you look for it.* If, for example, you lose your keys, you've got a reasonable chance of finding them.

Dave and I talked about how he didn't ever actually have the $200,000 and he had no chance at all of finding it if he went looking for it. So it wasn't lost, and telling himself it was lost only created stress and upset. A considerable drawback was that the stress and upset got in the way of doing what he could do (and needed to do) to make more sales.

Do you recall my telling about Claire?

Yes, she was the person you told me about in Chapter 2. Claire was referred to you by her supervisor. I think you said she was depressed and had a tough childhood.

That's right. Claire did a great deal of "lost" thinking. Because she so often told herself she had lost, she felt like a loser. She felt worthless. Her secret self-esteem was as low as her stress was high. What Claire told herself she had lost was a happy childhood and being loved as a child.

Claire didn't lose her happy childhood and the love; she didn't have it to lose. Even if she did have it, there was no way she could go out and find it. Agonizing over a childhood and love she didn't have just got in her way. If she were to keep that up, someday she would be agonizing over her lost adulthood.

What are some other things people do "lost" thinking about?

Those I hear the most are:

- Happy marriages.
- Death of a loved one.

The death of someone you love is a great loss. Anyone would feel that way.

People living in other cultures around the world don't do "lost" thinking when people die. Some of them celebrate death as a graduation to a better existence. One day I was talking to a client, and I made the comment that people suffer when someone they love dies. She immediately said, "I don't." Then she explained that because of her deep religious faith, she didn't feel a loss.

I understand what you're saying, but I'll need to think about this one some more. Are there other issues people tend to do "lost" thinking about?

I frequently hear about:

- Children who grow up.
- Motherhood or fatherhood.
- A romantic relationship.
- Money from stocks.
- Hair.
- Good looks.
- Youth.

But I thought you said "lost" thinking is believing you lost something you didn't have before. I certainly had my youth before. So I lost it, right?

I also said that if you lost something you had some chance of finding it again.

Racy Thinking

A great deal of stress occurs on streets and highways. One cause is what I've dubbed "racy thinking." Whenever you're in a hurry you're probably doing this duck-like thinking.

My own racy thinking became clear as Judy and I were returning home from a weekend trip to the beach. We'd been riding three hours. It was noon and past time for a "pit stop." I was feeling the effects of stress and didn't want to stop. I asked myself, "What might I be thinking?" Fairly quickly it came to me, "If I slow down or stop, I'll get behind the people I've passed. And I'll get home a half-hour later."

Once I became aware of what I was most likely thinking beneath the surface, I answered it with the truth: "What difference does it make if I get behind those other drivers and do get home a half-hour later? It doesn't matter. I'm not racing anyone and there's no prize worth stress, discomfort, or danger for getting home earlier." I decided to slow down and then stopped for a while.

When you're in a hurry and stressed, chances are you're doing racy thinking. You think, without realizing it, that you'll somehow lose if you get behind, and you'll feel like a loser.

It seems like these false ways of thinking could go on forever. When do we get to what to do about them and the bad effects they have?

We have covered a good deal. We've covered several quacked quotes that generate stress and threaten us. What we can do about them begins with the next chapter and continues through the remainder of the book.

Give yourself a pat on the back for thinking enough of yourself, your career, your relationships, and other people to stick with me this long.

7

How to Master Stress

*Exactly How to Deal with and
Prevent Your Negative Stress*

Now we'll talk specifically about what you can do to master your stress and free yourself of undesirable moods. There is no rigid order, top to bottom, of the ways to handle stress. I do believe, though, that one method, Stress and Mood Mastery Three-Part Process, deserves the top spot. The process is similar to those already published by Aaron Beck and David Burns, in their efforts to help people suffering with depression and anxiety. If you were to ask me for just one stress remedy that you could really get involved in and rely on for good results, I would tell you the Three-Part Process is the one.

Stress and Mood Mastery
Three-Part Process

We discussed earlier how the most effective thing we can possibly do to master stress is encourage BEING—being truthful, aware, self-responsible, in the here and now, and be-lieving. I call the method of reaching that BEING goal the Stress and Mood Mastery Three-Part Process.

How would you like to have a very wise teacher or friend who is consistently willing, ready, and able to help you make the right decisions and feel much better? Following the Stress and Mood Mastery Three-Part Process as it's described here is a way of creating such a wise friend. With practice, you'll find you are able to be that wonderful friend to yourself and give yourself the answers and comfort you need.

Besides being very effective, the Three-Part Process is surprisingly easy. It takes little time and minimal effort. Let's discuss the three steps.

1. *Identify your feeling (or emotion)* or *the situation you're in.* State the feeling or guess what it is. For example, "I'm angry." "I believe I'm depressed." "I'm discouraged." "I'm afraid or nervous." If your feeling is not so clear, give it a general description. "I'm upset." "I am hurt." "I'm really bothered." The general description will do nearly as well as the more specific one.

To better identify your emotion, you can notice some common physical clues: crying; pain in your stomach, neck, back, or head; cold or cool hands; flushed face; a light-headed feeling; tightness across your chest; a feeling that you aren't getting enough air; loss of energy (feeling tired when there isn't any good reason for it); damp palms or a general sweaty feeling; tight or tense muscles; face muscles set in a frown; breath that comes out as a sigh or moan; unusually fast or slow breathing (for no apparent cause); "butterflies" in your stomach.

How come there are so many reactions I might notice in my body that will help me to know I'm having a bad feeling?

Partly because different emotions tend to be associated with their own set of physical reactions coming from stress. For instance, anxiety or fear is often, but not always, associated with these reactions: hands cooler than usual, sweating, trouble breathing, muscle pain, "butterflies" in the stomach. Depression or sadness is often associated with reactions such as tiredness, frowns, sighs or groaning sounds, lack of sexual interest, eating too much or too little, and crying. Different people may have different physical responses to the same emotions. Each of us has a good many physical symptoms of emotions or moods to master.

An important element of this first part of the process is to identify, as well as you can, the situation that's associated with your mood or feeling. A few examples of situations are: being in heavy traffic, having someone criticize you, knowing there are many things you need to get done, doing something you later identify as a "mistake," recalling something "bad" that happened, or imagining something you don't want to happen in the future.

At certain times no particular situation will seem to be associated with a mood or excess stress that comes "out of the blue." But when you can identify a situation, you'll have some help to do the next part of the process.

2. *Become aware of what you're thinking.* Your thoughts (probably associated with the situation) account for your stress and emotion, not the situation you identified. That's important to remember. Also remember that subconscious thoughts happen without awareness, so you may well need to guess what they are.

I bet that'll be the hardest part for me: knowing what I'm thinking that's subconscious and is making my stress. How can I know what I'm thinking that's hidden anyway?

You may need to guess. Chances are that right now you're telling yourself you have to know for sure what it is. You don't; guessing is good enough. Your guesses about what you're thinking that creates your stress are more likely to be accurate than you can imagine. Let me give a personal example.

I told myself some time ago, "I'm angry [the feeling] and I'm riding behind someone in the passing lane. My level of stress is out of sight. The driver I'm behind is going about five miles under the speed limit, is not passing anyone, and is showing no interest in getting back into the right-hand lane of traffic [the situation]." I'd picked out what I was feeling and what the situation was (the first part of the process). Next, I needed to decide what I was thinking that I wasn't aware of.

My inclination was to tell myself I was simply thinking, "I'm riding behind a slow driver in the passing lane." But I knew that thought alone wouldn't produce such a strong feeling. So I asked myself, "What might I really be thinking?"

After briefly considering two or three possibilities, I decided I was probably thinking, "This person is driving slowly on purpose to get in the way of people like me who are in a hurry to get somewhere. She's trying to slow us down, so we'll be late. It's just not right [fair] for her to do that."

Thinking that some stranger was purposely attempting to slow me and other drivers down was a pretty "strange" thing to be thinking. It took some intestinal fortitude to admit it to myself. An important element of this part of the Stress and Mood Mastery Three-Part Process is to have the courage to be truthful with ourselves about what we might be thinking.

If you have much trouble with this part of the Three-Part Process, you probably haven't yet admitted what your thoughts actually are. Go ahead and be fully honest with yourself about what you may be thinking. No one will know but you.

But what if I'm thinking something really terrible, or stupid? Won't it make things worse to admit I'm thinking them?

Even if what you are thinking is, you believe, "terrible" or "stupid," your unhappiness, excess stress, hurt relationships, lack of greater success, poor health, or risk of poor health come from those secret thoughts. The only way to deal with them is to get them out into the open.

3. *Identify and counter duck-like thinking.* The third step of the Three-Part Process is to identify what you are thinking as being one (or possibly more) example of the duck thinking I described earlier. Counter it with the truth.

Using the example of someone driving slowly in the passing lane, I decided that the duck-like thinking I could have been using was "oughty." "She shouldn't [ought not to] be driving so slowly on a four-lane highway and especially not in the passing lane."

It could have been "oughty" thinking, but I decided later it was even more likely to be "I just know" thinking. What was probably going on in my head was more the thought, "*I just know* this old woman is trying to slow down drivers who are in a hurry. She probably thinks people drive too fast and she is doing her part to slow us down."

Couldn't you have been thinking that you were going to be late, instead of thinking the woman was trying to get in your way?

Yes, it could have been that. In this case it wasn't. Even if I were thinking I was going to be late it still would have been "I just know" thinking. "*I just know* I'm going to be late for my appointment."

Still, if you really were going to be late, wouldn't that be a bad thing? You'd have reason to be upset about that, it seems to me.

If I had been thinking I was going to be late and it was a bad thing, then I would have been using the quacked thinking I call "terrible" thinking. "Wouldn't it be terrible [bad] if I'm late for my meeting?" I couldn't know that it would be terrible. It might have turned out to be a good event in the long run. For example, by being late I might have avoided a deadly traffic accident.

In that example you gave before about the slow driver, you said you didn't think it was right for her to be doing that. Could you have been doing "it's not fair" thinking? It's not fair she's driving so slow in the passing lane.

That's true. It could have been "it's not fair." Often there is more than one possibility. I'm impressed you picked that up so soon.

As important as it is to get a good idea of what inaccurate thought you might be having, it's even more important to do the next part, to answer or counter the untruthful thinking you were probably doing subconsciously and weren't aware of before. To give you the skill and confidence to start countering untrue thinking in your own words, the list of quacked quotes in Chapters 5 and 6 is repeated here with a "possible counter" for each kind of thinking. As you read the possible counters, think about how you would answer in your own words. Your chance is coming!

1. *"Makes Me Feel" Thinking*

We may mistakenly believe that someone or something can cause us to experience stress or feel something. For example: "He makes me so angry. My job makes me so stressed out."

Possible Counter: "No one and nothing stresses me or makes me feel something. It is what I believe is (or may be) true that decides my level of stress or how I feel. No one pours stress or feelings into me. What comes out of me is what's inside of me, and what's inside is created by my thoughts, by my interpretation of what is going on or has happened. Taking credit for my stress and how I feel is the truthful, aware, and self-responsible thing to do."

2. *"Makes Me Do" Thinking*

When we say words like "have to, gotta, must, got no choice," we have our "minds in the gotta." We are saying we have no option but to do, think, or feel something.

Possible Counter: "There's a choice. Even if I don't like the choice, the truth is that it's there anyway. It's important that I take responsibility for myself. I am a worthy adult and saying 'I have to' denies that."

If you have trouble understanding these brief descriptions of duck-like thinking and possible counters, refer to the full explanations earlier in the book.

---

3. *Oughty Thoughts*

Using words such as "should, ought to, shouldn't, ought not" is oughty thinking. It implies there's some unbreakable and universally accepted set of rules we and others are required to obey. People who use such words are (usually unknowingly) setting themselves up as superior persons/authorities/parent-figures.

Possible Counter: "The fact is there aren't any 'shoulds, oughts,' and so on, because there isn't any absolute, unbreakable, and universally accepted set of rules people live by. I can talk and think in terms of something being *important* to consider or something I (or others) *need* to consider. Those are more likely to be facts. Also, I don't want to set myself up as superior or as a negative parent-figure. When I do that with myself or others, I encourage that part of myself that robs me of happiness. And I encourage others and myself to behave poorly and immaturely."

4. *"It's Not Fair" Thinking*

Being upset because someone, life, the government, or whatever didn't or doesn't treat us fairly is based on the subconscious and false belief that life is like a game with definite rules that are commonly understood and agreed upon. Also, "it's not fair" thinking implies that others "should" do what's in our best interest or do as we think is "right." It's very child-like thinking. This mallard muttering is too often a marriage killer.

Possible Counter: "Life is life, not a game where all is supposed to be fair. Life is for living rather than for playing at living. Other people will most likely do what they believe is in their best interest. That's the way things are, and all the not-liking-it in the world will do nothing to change it. If anything can be done to remedy what I used to call "unfair," I'm much more likely to do it when I am free of useless stress and upset I give myself over things not being 'fair.' I need to shine my light at my feet, rather than expecting others to light the path for me."

5. *"Making Magic" Thinking*

Another name for this thinking is worrying—needless thoughts about something negative that might happen or has already happened. We learn nothing from worrying and are not planning or evaluating. Unknown to us, we think that by worrying we will magically show affection, or influence the past or future.

Possible Counter: "Worrying is the magic thinking of childhood, and I'm grown up now. Worrying is shining my light anywhere but at my feet, where it needs to be. By stopping my worrying I can pay attention to what really matters: what I can do in the here and now."

6. *"Can't" Thinking*

When we say "can't," we're literally stating that something isn't possible, that there are no options or alternatives to some particular course of action.

Possible Counter: "I avoid saying 'can't' because it is so rarely true and it denies my responsibility. What 'I can't' probably means is, 'I don't like the alternatives and don't want to take responsibility.' The truth is: I can, and it is my responsibility."

7. *"I Just Know" Thinking*

When we think "I just know" what's going to happen or what someone else is thinking, we're pretending to be a fortune teller or mind
reader. We are telling ourselves that we're not just guessing but
actually know for sure. This is a favorite way of thinking for those
who experience much fear, tension, panic, or anxiety. Someone who
is afraid almost certainly does this duck-like thinking.

Possible Counter: "Only fortune tellers have signs with red
hands on them in their front yards. I have no such sign. I do not tell
fortunes or read minds. I don't know for sure what's going to happen
or what people are thinking even after they tell me. Guessing—even
good guessing—is not knowing. I keep my light at my feet and feel
loved, calm, and safe."

8. *"Grate Expectations" Thinking*

We often expect more than is reasonable from others and ourselves.
Being angry (fear with a mean face) at ourselves or others is often a
signal that this is happening.

Possible Counter: "I expect from myself and others what's reasonable. I know I'm doing that, in part, because I'm not angry at
myself and others. If I need more consideration from others, I can
constructively confront."

9. *Faulty Thinking: Placing Blame*

Placing fault or blame encourages guilt in ourselves and others and
uses that guilt to try to manipulate, control, or attack. It's a way of
(1) avoiding taking responsibility for ourselves or (2) taking more
responsibility than is reasonable, "It's all my fault."

Possible Counter: "I'm worthwhile no matter what I do, and so
are others. I don't need to try to prove my value by finding fault with
others. I am of great value. It's enough for me to know that. Blaming
myself does no more good than blaming others. I take responsibility
for what's happening now. That's right to do and that's enough."

10. *"Don't Like" Thinking*

Saying "I don't like" means we think what we do or don't like
matters most. This thinking implies that what we do or whom we
associate with is rightfully determined by what we like or don't like
(want). For example, if we say, "I don't like to exercise," we are
saying that our not liking it is more important than the fact that
exercise likes us.

Possible Counter: "When liking is defined as being protective and helpful, what matters most is what likes me. I deserve the liking offered me by whatever or whoever likes me. My task is to keep on liking myself. And I do good things for myself, whether I 'like' to or not."

11. "What People Say Matters Most" Thinking

This duck-like thinking leads us to believe people typically say what they mean, and we take what people say at face value. If people use words that are critical of us or make fun of us, then we mistakenly believe they think there is something wrong with us and they don't like us.

Possible Counter: "It is safest to assume that when I'm upset or hurt I don't yet understand what's meant by what is said or written. When I do understand, I'll feel all right or even good."

12. "Get Even" Thinking

Trying to get even or having the urge to do so comes out of a false belief, left over from childhood, that life is actually a game or war. When we believe that people who have "hurt" or "offended" us have not suffered sufficiently for it, we take it upon ourselves to punish them by getting back at them. Such mallard mumblings are the stuff that cripple and even destroy relationships, especially marriages.

Possible Counter: "Life is for living instead of playing at living. I want my life to be happy and free of needless stress, and playing hurtful games or making war isn't going to make it that way. Those who try to hurt me (actually no one can hurt me, except physically) will suffer more from their messed-up thinking than from anything I could ever do to them."

13. "Always/Never" Thinking

This is thinking in absolutes, and absolutes are extremely rare. Words like "always, never, just like, every time, all, everyone, and nobody" express absolutes. Since absolutes are so very often untrue, we encourage others and our own subconscious minds to mistrust us when we use them. That's hurtful, and we deserve much better.

Possible Counter: "Because I want to build trust and know and tell the truth, I avoid absolutes. To use an absolute is most likely to tell a lie. I am an eagle thinker and talker. I think and tell the truth."

14. *"If Only" Thinking*

Wishing, or thinking "If only . . . ," is a childhood "answer" to an adult's world. It's no real answer at all because it denies truth, good awareness, and self-responsibility. It's living away from the here and now and denying the reality of what's going on.

Possible Counter: "I'm an adult and no longer wish. I *make* my life better, instead of trying to wish it so."

15. *"I Can Make Up For" Thinking*

To believe we can magically make up for what we think, or know, we missed out on earlier in life is duck thinking. Perhaps we think we can make up for love, experiences, food, attention, or approval we didn't get from others.

Possible Counter: "Life isn't a test I can make up later. Trying to make up for something takes away the only life I have—that which is going on right now. I keep my flashlight on my feet; I live and make better use of the life I have."

16. *"I'm My Shirt" Thinking*

Confusing what we do, think, or feel with what we truly are is "I'm my shirt" thinking. For example, "If I do something bad, then I am bad."

Possible Counter: "Since what I truly am is perfect (perfectly me), my behavior, thoughts, and feelings aren't required to be perfect. Changing behavior is necessary the way changing a smelly shirt is necessary. Still, I'm not my shirt. I'm worthwhile no matter what."

17. *Hindsight-Labels Thinking*

Placing negative labels such as "bad" or "stupid" on ourselves or what we've done is self-criticism and self-punishment. It seriously hurts our secret self-esteem.

Possible Counter: "Calling myself bad names hurts how I feel about me. How I feel about me determines how well I can treat myself and others. I improve my ability to love and treat others well by avoiding calling myself negative names."

18. *"Terrible" Thinking*

When we place negative labels such as "terrible, horrible, the worst, a nightmare" on what happens in our lives, our bodies respond with considerable and needless stress.

Possible Counter: "The only happenings in life that are truly 'terrible' are those that will have no positive outcome. Since I don't know for sure whether there will be a positive or negative outcome, it makes no sense to think of anything as 'terrible.'" Remember the story about the horse running away.

19. *"Yes, But" Thinking*

When we agree with something and then say "but," it's likely that we don't truly believe (subconsciously) what we agreed with. We are trying to hold on to an untruth and don't realize it.

Possible Counter: "I just agreed with something and then said, 'but.' Chances are, at a deeper level, I don't believe what I agreed to. I need to examine that possibility."

20. *"Don't" Thinking*

Disagreeing quickly with some authority (in person, on an audio tape, or in a book) that you have gone to for advice or for analysis of a problem is a poor attempt to build your secret self-esteem.

Possible Counter: "I'm already of the greatest value. If someone knows more than I, it doesn't detract from my worth. Simply and quickly disagreeing with someone in authority proves nothing. I don't know yet, but the prospects are that what I've been told is true. My stress level and happiness deserve the benefits gained by waiting and giving it serious thought."

21. *"I'll Do Better When" Thinking*

When we postpone exercising, eating nutritious foods, or doing anything else that benefits (likes) us, we're doing this kind of duck-like thinking—an indication that we are probably addicted.

Possible Counter: "I deserve better now! I'm just kidding myself and shining my light away from my feet when I say I'll do better later. I need to examine the prospect that I'm addicted."

22. *"Poor Me" Thinking*

We tell ourselves "poor me" when we feel victimized or deprived for some reason: we were raised in a poor family, or we were abused, or we have some physical deformity or a disease. The possibilities are considerable.

Possible Counter: "I'm just doing 'poor me' thinking. Feeling sorry for myself and having a 'pity party' doesn't do any good. Besides, what has happened has not affected my value as a person. I only have a legitimate reason to feel sorry for myself when my value as a person is damaged. Of course, that will not happen."

23. Duck-Plays-Ostrich Thinking

These false thoughts say that not knowing is somehow better than knowing what's going on. For example, people who don't keep their checking balance accurate and up-to-date are thinking this way. "If I don't know how much money is in the account, it's probably enough."

Possible Counter: "I keep my head out of the sand and get the information I need. Knowing is so much better than not knowing."

24. "Luck" (Sounds like Duck) Thinking

When we think that the "bad" or "good" events that happen are caused by luck, that's "Luck" (sounds like duck) thinking. It comes, as do the other faulty ways of thinking, from hurt self-esteem. On one hand, it denies our responsibility for happenings we identify as "bad." It also denies our efforts in creating what we call "good." ("How could a worthless person like me make such good things happen?")

Possible Counter: "Luck really does sound like duck. I'm responsible, but not to blame, for things that happen that I don't like. I'm equally responsible for what happens that I do like. It's me, not luck."

25. "It's Too Hard" Thinking

Some people mistakenly believe that challenges experienced in living happen to (and hard work is done by) those who are inferior. So, if they need to overcome obstacles or work hard to succeed, they may think (and don't realize it) that they're somehow inferior. That misconception of being inferior leads to much dangerous stress.

Possible Counter: "The greater the challenges and the harder I work, the better the ultimate outcome. If it doesn't seem that way, I just haven't given it enough time. How hard I work and challenges I experience say nothing at all about my value. I'm of the greatest value."

26. "Lost" Thinking

We create stress and upset when we tell ourselves we lost something we didn't have before or have no chance of finding. Happy childhood, love, and children who grow up are just a few examples.

Possible Counter: "If I think about losing, I only make myself feel like a loser. And I'm not a loser! I don't lose something I never had. Besides, I'm not about to find it again. So why bother looking?"

27. Racy Thinking

When we're in a hurry and stressed, we're probably doing racy thinking. We think, without realizing it, that we'll somehow lose if we get behind. And "losing," we'll feel like a loser. We mistakenly believe that our hurt secret self-esteem is confirmed.

Possible Counter: "Life isn't a race to win or lose. I'm a winner already, whether I fully accept it yet or not. There's no need to race to try to prove I'm a winner, not a loser."

Getting Back to the Example

Let's use again the example of my driving behind a slow driver. I recognized what I was thinking as being "I just know" thinking. "I'm doing 'I just know' thinking: I know she is trying to slow me down. The fact is that I don't have a mind reader's sign in my front yard. There's no way I can know for sure what this woman driver is thinking. Perhaps there's less traffic in this lane, and so she is attempting to stay out of other people's way. She may be frightened of the traffic and just doesn't know (or her fear overrules what she knows) the law that says slow vehicles are to be driven in the right-hand lane. My best bet is to not encourage her fear and either ride a safe distance behind her or pass her carefully on the right."

Writing the Three–Part Process

It seems to me that I've done what you're suggesting, and it hasn't helped. I've told myself that I'm not thinking accurately and I should be thinking something else. But it's hard to always do that.

I'm glad you brought this up. People have known for many years that writing something down can be extremely helpful to learning and understanding. For most of us, simply thinking something isn't nearly enough. The thought doesn't sink in and make a great difference until we write it down.

Much of this has to do with how we learn. What we *hear*, from ourselves or others, helps with short-term learning and comprehension. What we *see* helps with long-term learning or memory and has a longer lasting effect.

The accuracy of what we remember is greatly affected by the accuracy of our thinking. The more accurate our thinking, the more accurate our memories. Duck thinking produces duck memories.

Our mind alters our memories to fit what we believe is true. That's part of the reason two people can have such differing recollections of the same event.

If your memory of something differs considerably from someone else's, consider which of you is more the eagle thinker. Assume the variance in your thinking, rather than lying, is the explanation for what happened.

By writing down the three parts of the Stress and Mood Mastery Three-Part Process, you'll gain much more than long-lasting benefits. You'll clarify your thinking and get to the heart of your thoughts. A great writer once said, "How can I know what I think, until I write it down and read it?"

I strongly encourage you to write down the Three-Part Process, for a far greater and more lasting effect and unbelievable benefits to you.

Some examples of my own use of this process will help you get started. These are just a few of my personal experiences over several years. I've expanded on them a bit so you'll be better able to learn from them.

Remember that Part One of the process requires identifying the uncomfortable feeling and/or the situation you are in. Part Two determines what you are thinking that's subconscious or what you might be thinking. Part Three decides which one (often more than one) of the duckish ways of thinking might fit. In your own words, you'll counter it with reason, with the truth as well as you can determine it.

*   *   *

Part One. (Identify your feeling and/or the situation you are in.) "I am tense. The funny feeling in my stomach and the hurting muscles between my shoulder blades help me to know that. I'm feeling a lot of stress. My appointment book is full . . . too full . . . and I'm only one-third of the way through the day."

Part Two. (Become aware of, or guess at, what you are really thinking.) "I'm most likely thinking, 'This is just too much. I *can't* see so many people today.'"

Part Three. (Identify and counter duck thinking.) "I am doing "can't" thinking. It could also be 'I don't like' thinking as in, 'I don't like seeing so many clients in one day.' But I think it is more likely 'can't' thinking.

"The problem is that I'm shining my flashlight too far down the path. I'm trying to do the full day of work all at one time. I can handle what I need to, and do it well, in manageable parts; I'll take one client at a time. I need to keep my light at my feet.

"Still further, the truth is that I can see these clients. It simply isn't true that I can't."

*   *   *

Part One. "A new client hasn't shown up for an appointment. I'm angry."

Part Two. "My anger isn't caused by the person not keeping his appointment. It is caused by thinking that this is not *fair*. It is only right for this person to treat me fairly and at least call and cancel this appointment, rather than let me sit here waiting for him to show up."

Part Three. "Fair is the place where they have the ferris wheel. The client who didn't keep his appointment is doing what he believes is in his best interest right now. That's what human beings do. My getting angry because a human is being human simply isn't reasonable. It's duck thinking: 'it's not fair' thinking.

"Instead of wasting my time being angry (it's really fear with a mean face anyway), I'll spend it doing something else here in the office that needs to be done. I'll take advantage of the free time and turn it into an asset, as I've done before. Also, I'll do my best to contact this client to let him know that I care about him and am willing to see him."

*   *   *

Part One. "I haven't exercised in days, and I'm upset (angry) with me."

Part Two. "Most likely, I'm thinking that I *should* have exercised. I am getting after myself for not doing what I know is in my best interest."

Part Three. "This is 'oughty' (should) thinking. Since I'm not a child, it isn't appropriate for me to treat myself like a child. Besides, in treating myself like a child I only encourage myself to act child-like and rebel against myself. I don't want to do that.

"The truth is I *need* to exercise and *deserve* it and the benefits I get from it. What I need to do is remind myself that I do need exercise and avoid pushing myself to do it. I may also need to investigate what's holding me back.

"One of the things holding me back may be that I've been thinking 'I'll do better when' thinking. The time to treat me better is now. I do what I do that is in my best interest—what is positive—because I am worth it!"

*   *   *

Part One. "I'm stressed and upset. Judy [my wife] is quiet and aloof."

Part Two. "I am telling myself she is angry at me, and I don't know what I've done to make her angry."

Part Three. "I am doing 'I just know' thinking: 'I just know Judy is upset with me.' Judy may be angry but I don't know that she's angry with me. Besides, it is impossible for me to 'make her feel' upset. As is the case with me, what she thinks decides what she feels. Right now she may be thinking duck. It isn't appropriate for me to point that out to her, however, unless she asks me to.

"Maybe I'll ask her if there is some way I can help."

*   *   *

Part One. "I'm angry with myself. The reason is that I got angry at Brian [my teenage son] earlier and made some critical comments."

Part Two. "It's likely I'm thinking, 'I shouldn't get angry at Brian.'" [I probably had a "grate expectation" of him.]

Part Three. "I am having an oughty thought. Doing duck thinking now because I did duck thinking earlier (with Brian) and acted accordingly isn't reasonable. I am perfect (perfectly me) even if I don't behave perfectly. I can change my behavior (like my shirt) and I intend to do so. I will apologize to Brian and stop having a 'grate expectation' of myself—that I'll never make a mistake."

Anger (loud fear or fear with a mean face) is often a useless emotion. It took me many years to come to that realization. As we learn to master our stress we feel less and less the need to experience and express anger.

Part of my realization of anger's uselessness came from an unusual source. I was watching a movie starring Bruce Lee, a famous martial artist. Bruce was teaching a student how to spar (pretend fighting). He asked the student to spar "with feeling." Subsequently, the student angrily responded to Bruce's "attack." Bruce reprimanded him, "I said with feeling, not with anger." To me, he was saying it was possible to respond to threat with an emotion, other than anger, that comes out of skill. It might be called "intensity" or "purposefulness," but it isn't anger.

Fear (in the form we usually experience it) may well be as unnecessary, for many of us, as anger is. When I, for example, told a woman with a phobia (very strong irrational fear) of high places that with stress mastery she could be rid of the phobia for good, she said, "But what will keep me from going and standing on a construction beam 20 floors up?" I told her, "Your good sense to avoid such places and the fact that you care about yourself and your safety."

Practicing the Process

To make the best possible use of this new learning, you need to begin right away to use it. Before going any further, take some paper and a pen and begin to practice using the Three-Part Process. Recall situations, no matter how insignificant, in which you felt excess stress or bad moods. Maybe someone got your parking place, your child was slow getting ready for school, your boss criticized you, you spilled a cup of coffee.

Please note: To get this far, you've shown a strong interest in further improving the quality and conditions of your life by mastering your stress. You've also shown excellent potential to be a true stress master, an eagle thinker to the highest degree. You're at a crucial point in this book and possibly in your life: Will you go beyond a strong interest and excellent potential? You do that by beginning now—not later today, or tomorrow, but right now—to practice the Three-Part Process in writing. Doing it in your head isn't enough at first. Don't be concerned about how well you do it or even how much you do it. Just do it very soon because you will be beginning a process that's larger and more important than the Three-Part Process. Once begun, the larger process will effectively control your stress, obvious and hidden, and enhance your secret self-esteem.

What follows are only some samples of what you might write.

* * *

Part One. Identify the situation you are in and (if possible) the feeling you experience in relation to the situation.

I was going to work this morning and felt bad—maybe nervous.

Part Two. What do you know or suspect you are thinking in relation to the above situation? Be very honest with yourself.

It could have been that I would get to work and there would be a great deal of work to get done and people pushing me to do it right away.

Part Three. What category of duck thinking is the thinking in Part Two? What is the accurate (eagle) thinking you use to counter the duck thinking?

Chances are, Part Two is "I just know" thinking. I just know I'll get to work and there will be too much to do. The accurate thinking is that I'm not a fortune teller. Even if there was too much work every day for a year, there's still no way I can be certain the same will be a fact today. Guessing isn't knowing. Making myself tense and upset before I even get started isn't helping even a little. I'll concentrate on getting to work safely—keeping my light at my feet, where it needs to be.

* * *

Part One. Identify the situation you are in and (if possible) the feeling you experience in relation to the situation.

My daughter was crying over nothing at all, and I got after her about it. I yelled and was angry.

Part Two. What do you know or suspect you are thinking in relation to the above situation? Be very honest with yourself.

She makes me so mad sometimes. Here I am trying to get ready to go and she's crying and slowing me down.

Part Three. What category of duck thinking is the thinking in Part Two? What is the accurate (eagle) thinking you use to counter the duck thinking?

Since I wrote that she made me mad, I'm doing "makes me feel" thinking. The reality is that she absolutely didn't make me angry, any more than I'm from Mars. What I was thinking and didn't even know about made me mad. Chances are that I also had a "grate expectation" of her. I was expecting her to act more like an adult when she isn't one. She's a child. That's okay.

*   *   *

Part One. Identify the situation you are in and, if possible, the feeling you experience in relation to the situation.

This afternoon, I went to the grocery store and was about to check out. I got in the shortest line. It turned out to be the slowest line. People who got in the longer lines got out of the store before me. I'm frustrated.

Part Two. What do you know or suspect you are thinking in relation to the above situation? Be very honest with yourself.

It never fails. No matter what I do, I screw up and choose the wrong line. Dummy.

Part Three. What category of duck thinking is the thinking in Part Two? What is the accurate (eagle) thinking you use to counter the duck thinking?

There are two different duck-like thoughts going on here. The first is always/never thinking. I said that it never fails that I get in the wrong line. That's not a fact. Sometimes I get in the faster line, but those times are evidently harder to recall. I'll like me better and trust me better by telling myself the truth: I don't always make the wrong choices.

The second duck-like way of thinking is "I'm my shirt" thinking. Because I made the wrong choice about the lines in the store, I'm telling myself I was bad or dumb. My choices are behaviors and are like my shirt. It's not me, so I won't get after myself.

*   *   *

Part One. Identify the situation you are in and, if possible, the feeling you experience in relation to the situation.

> *I found myself feeling sad. It came from nowhere, for no reason I could put my finger on. There wasn't any particular situation, but the stress and sadness were there anyway.*

Part Two. What do you know or suspect you are thinking in relation to the above situation? Be very honest with yourself.

> *Work has been a little slow lately and probably I've worried about that. Could be I was thinking, and didn't even know it, that this is a bad thing and it's going to get even worse.*

Part Three. What category of duck thinking is the thinking in Part Two? What is the accurate (eagle) thinking you use to counter the duck thinking?

> *Some of the duck-like thinking is "terrible" thinking, as in "This is terrible or bad that work is slow." There's just no way on God's green earth that I can judge something until it's over. It's hard to imagine, but it might turn out to be a blessing.*
>
> *Also, I'm doing "I just know" thinking. I just know that this is going to get worse. Boy, do I need to keep my light at my feet and stop thinking I can see up the path accurately and know what's going to happen before it happens. Guessing still isn't knowing.*

Streams of Thought

A very important fact to understand is that, except when we're asleep, we are continually thinking on at least two levels of our mind. We are thinking *conscious thoughts* and at the same time we are thinking *subconscious thoughts*. Our subconscious thoughts can affect us far more than our conscious thoughts. Let me give an example.

* * *

Conscious Stream of Thought. "Let's see, I need to go to the bank and. . . ."

At the level of conscious awareness, thoughts here are concerned with errands we need to do during the day, such as go to the bank.

Subconscious Stream of Thought. "If I forget to do something, it means *I'm stupid.* I've *got to* remember everything. I *can't* do anything right. I *must* do everything I set out to do or *I'm no good.* . . ."

Because of the subconscious stream of thought and all of its negatives (mallard mumblings) we find ourselves needlessly tense as we set out to get some errands done. And we don't know why we're tense (stressed).

*   *   *

What this example is leading up to is that we can, to a great extent, counteract what's going on in the subconscious stream of thought. By counteracting it, we feel happier and more comfortable. We are freer of stress.

Using Affirmations

An excellent way to help counteract is to regularly use affirmations: usually short, positive statements. Repeated review of affirmations will get them into your subconscious stream of thinking just like the duck-like thinking got there: through repeated use.

I can suggest a few affirmations for you, but the better ones will be those you come up with yourself. Here are a few of my recommendations.

- More and more, I'm a stress master.
- When I think the truth, I am happier.
- The more I know me, the more I love me.
- What I think decides what I feel.
- I am an eagle thinker.
- I do good and have good things, because I deserve them.
- I shine my flashlight at my feet and understand when others do the same.
- I am entirely responsible for what happens in my life.
- What and who truly likes, protects, and helps me matters more than what and who I like.
- I approve of myself; others need to do the same for themselves.
- Life is full of opportunity instead of fairness.

- I am worth what it takes to have success, a good life, good physical and mental well-being, and satisfying relationships.
- My capacity for no-matter-what love of others grows with my willingness to love myself unconditionally.

What Is True Love?

Love for others is a wonderful feeling we can share with others, because we have it for ourselves. Until we have it for ourselves, we do not truly have it for others. We may be attracted to others, we may need them, we may even be addicted to them, and we may relieve needless guilt by doing things for them, but we do not yet love them.

Not loving ourselves is very "self-centered." It keeps us from giving love to others. So, stop being so "self-centered!"

- I am important and perfect even when I do, think, or feel things that aren't perfect.
- I am an eagle thinker, I fill myself with eagle thoughts and talk.
- When I have success, money, and more, it's because I deserve them. And I deserve them even before I get them.
- I am forgiven and I now forgive everyone in my past, present, and future.
- When it is to be, it is up to me.
- As I think more of me, I think more of others.

Some of these sayings—these affirmations—feel okay when you say them. Others bother me. It's just hard for me to tell myself I'm perfect or I love me.

You probably need to put into your stream of subconscious thoughts those affirmations that you don't (right now) find comfortable. Those are likely the ones most *unlike* the thoughts continually going on in your subconscious. That difference explains the discomfort.

The next most important affirmations are those you feel most comfortable with. You already recognize them, at a deeper level of thinking, as being needed.

Make good use of affirmations; the more you review them, the better! Remember, it takes plenty of repetition to get them into the subconscious flow of thought so that they can increasingly equal out and eventually override your duck-like thinking there.

One of the best ways to get this done is to have lists of affirmations in places where you can regularly, conveniently, and safely review them. A good time to review affirmations in your car is when you stop at a traffic signal; attach them to your sun visor. (Please do not review affirmations while driving.) Underline or put a check beside the affirmations you need to concentrate most on, but don't ignore the others. You can later add other affirmations that you discover.

From the affirmations on your list, you may later come to realize that a particular continuing and hurtful statement is going on subconsciously. I'll give a personal example. As I began to use the Stress and Mood Mastery Three-Part Process, I realized that I sometimes made reference to my intelligence. I would make statements like "Boy, that was stupid." "I'm a real dummy." "That was so silly of me." (All were examples of "hindsight-labels" thinking.)

Because I had difficulty as a student early in my life, I had interpreted that as meaning I wasn't bright. It wasn't until I had completed requirements for my doctorate that I fully realized this inaccurate thinking.

Stopping Duck Thinking with Affirmations

At times our conscious thinking can seem to get stuck on a "mallard muttering" that creates stress and worry. Perhaps our child stays out too late, or finances take a turn for the worse. We find it difficult to get away from thoughts such as, "I just know something bad has happened to my child." "This financial trouble is so bad [terrible]."

The truth contained in affirmations is a wonderful antidote for the untruths we tell ourselves. When our falsehoods to ourselves are conscious and intense, as when we're worrying, we need a heavy dose of written affirmations. I call this an *"I Choose Truth List."*

To make an I Choose Truth List you can carry with you and refer to often, take an index card or piece of paper and write at the top of it, "I choose truth." Then write two or more truths/affirmations. You might write:

- When I know the truth, I feel good.
- I shine my light at my feet.
- I am worth what it takes to stay calm.

I didn't say this before when you were talking about affirmations and making lists and putting them where I could see them. Now you're talking about this choosing truth list that I should carry with me. I guess you want me to read it over and over when I'm worrying, to stop that thinking. The thing is that using these affirmations seems so sappy to me. I mean, I'd feel like some kind of idiot to be reading those sweet little sayings.

Do you believe that I am a sap or idiot for using affirmations?

No, I guess not.

Do you think that other people who have used and mastered their stress with affirmations were saps or idiots for doing that?

No. It worked for them, but I just don't think it would do anything for me except make me feel foolish.

Remember, you have no sign with a red hand on it in your front yard. You aren't a fortune teller. You are unable to know in advance whether affirmations will help. Also, using affirmations cannot *make you* feel foolish. If you feel foolish, it's because you already have duck thinking that you don't know about yet. Using affirmations can help get at those thoughts and get them out.

I suspect that nearly all of us at first feel uncomfortable with affirmations, or just don't have any real interest in them, because affirmations don't reflect what's going on in our subconscious mind. Our subconscious has too few positives, little optimism and less truth, and practically no good statements about us. Affirmations are just the opposite; that's why they feel out of place and uncomfortable. We explain this discomfort in the best way we can (but inaccurately) by saying things such as, "Affirmations are so sappy." "I just don't think they would do me any good." "Using them just doesn't interest me." "It doesn't make sense to me." "I don't understand how it can possibly help." "I'll do them later."

I strongly recommend you give affirmations at least a chance to be helpful—to help you to be more and more a stress master by counteracting negatives in your subconscious stream of thought. On as many days as you can, and at different times of the day, read and think about the affirmations. Post them where you can see them and review them. If you find you tend to worry or get stressed because you keep on thinking something, make an I Choose Truth List and counteract the worry or stress by focusing on eagle thinking (the truth).

Notice What You Say (Duck Dialogue)

What we say aloud to others, and what we say to ourselves in "self-talk," reflects what's going on in our subconscious stream of thought. Particular words are an integral part of duck thinking and when we notice those words we can strongly suspect that duck thinking is going on. Here are some common words that indicate duck-like thinking.

Duck Dialogue

makes me	always	pull my strings
got to (gotta)	just like	push my buttons
have to	worry	luck
must	(do) better	fail
ought	wish	don't like
should	(yes) but	if only
cannot	expect	terrible
can't	poor me	awful
just know	get even	lost
fair	make up for	used me
every	fault	hurry
all	blame	too hard
never		dumb

The more you and I can get words such as these out of our talk to ourselves and others, the more we are thinking truthfully—the more we are doing eagle thinking. (MentaLinguistics is the term I created to indicate that a purposeful and constructive shift in language yields a corresponding shift in attitude or thinking.)

I don't know how much good it'll do to change my words.

You'll be mentally and physically stronger. When I do seminars, I often ask for a volunteer, to help me demonstrate something interesting. First, I ask her (or him) to hold her arm out to her side. Then I ask her to think of the word "free" and to keep thinking of that word as I try to press her arm down. The volunteer typically has little trouble resisting me.

I let her rest her arm, and then I ask her to hold her arm out as before. This time I ask her to think of the word "quit" as I press her arm down (no harder than before). To her amazement, she finds that her arm is weaker. She has much more trouble keeping it up. She was stronger when she thought of the word "free." Each time, the word she was thinking as I pressed her arm down made the difference.

Have you ever noticed that the more you thought of "quitting," "stopping," or "giving up" something (perhaps smoking, or eating certain foods), the weaker you got—and the more you smoked or ate, or wanted to?

Yes, I believe I have noticed that.

The fact is, negative words that I call "quitter quotes" had a weakening effect on you. You'll do much better by telling yourself, and others, that you're "free" or "getting free" of whatever negative you're encountering, and you intend to stay "free" forever. The highly positive word "free" will have a strengthening effect on your resolutions. Your willpower will soar. Beginning now, avoid thinking and talking about quitting, stopping, or giving up anything. Think and talk about getting and staying *"free"* of it. Words such as "free" are what I call "winner words." *You're a winner, so use the words that fit you best.*

Famous people such as Mohandas Gandhi and Eleanor Roosevelt, who were known for clear thinking, truthfulness, or doing wonderful services for humanity, used very few duck dialogue terms. In fact they used about one-fifth as much duck dialogue as infamous people such as Adolf Hitler and Joseph Stalin. Hitler and Stalin were definitely not known for clear thinking, truthfulness, or helping others.

My data on their use of duck dialogue come from a computer-aided study of randomly selected writings of famous and infamous people. Although a small sample was researched, the inference is clear: *The more importance you place on the truth, the more clearly*

*you think, and the greater your love of others, the more your words will
reflect those qualities.*

Use Your Imagination

Our subconscious mind accepts as reality what we imagine. The better we imagine, the more likely it is to be accepted. For instance, think of yourself at a fair or amusement park, standing in front of a large roller coaster. Now imagine getting on the roller coaster and sitting in the front car. You lower the metal bar that holds you in place. The cars suddenly jerk and begin to roll forward. Think of yourself in the front car, rolling higher and higher, climbing still higher and higher toward the top of the highest hill. As clearly as you can, imagine your front car very near the top of that highest roller coaster hill. Now you are right at the verge of going over. Close your eyes for a moment as you vividly imagine yourself in the roller coaster car dropping over the crest of that hill and going nearly straight down, very fast.

Did you notice a physical reaction? Perhaps a bit of funny feeling in your stomach? Whether you could tell it or not, your body began to react to what you were imagining, as though you were actually there. You were being prepared physically for the more "threatening" part of a roller coaster ride. You created physical stress for yourself.

This is a simple example of how our subconscious mind responds well to what's imagined. We can use the same process increasingly to master our stress, to achieve greater success, and to be relieved of hurtful moods. Now, I want to make some recommendations about some things you can imagine.

- Think of two knobs on a radio. Imagine the radio and the knobs as clearly as you can. What comes to your mind as being accurate is accurate. Now imagine that one knob is labeled "duck thinking" and the other knob is labeled "eagle thinking." Think of yourself as reaching out and turning down the volume of duck thinking and then turning up the volume of eagle thinking.

DUCK   EAGLE

- Imagine yourself walking along a path in the forest and very purposefully bringing the beacon of your flashlight back to the ground near your feet. You're stepping safely and easily over obstacles in the path. You may see the words "love," "peaceful," and "calm" written there at your feet.

Stress and Mood Mastery
Verbal Interaction Model

The triangle at the top of the model shown on page 147 represents the part of our personality that we get by observing and imitating grownups, authority figures, when we are children. This part of ourselves is labeled *Authority Self.* The uppermost part of the triangle is the most untrue and negative.

The triangle at the bottom of the model, the *Immature Self,* stands for the part of our personality that's childlike. The lower portion is the most untrue and negative.

The middle section of the model, the *True Self,* represents what we actually are: truthful, responsible, aware, living in the here and now, and believing.

In the left column of the model are comments that might be made by the various "selves" to someone else. In the right column are examples of statements we might make to ourselves.

- Think about the model on page 147. Now picture yourself moving to the center part of your personality, your True Self. To do that more easily, you can think of yourself on a floor

Stress and Mood Mastery Verbal Interaction Model

Statements to Others		Statements to Ourselves
You are no good. You always (never, etc.) . . . . You really messed up. You can't. You have to. You shouldn't do that. I don't think you're right.	**Authority**	I must be inferior. I am angry at myself. I behaved terribly. I deserve punishment. I always do so poorly. I'm stupid. I shouldn't.

You should do that.
I'll take care of you.
I hope you have good
    luck.
You did really well.
I'll love you even
    better when . . . .
Do this right now.
	Self	I'll be careful not to fail.
		I did well that time, and so
		    I'm good.
		I like me because I did well.
		I'll give myself a treat for
		    doing so well.
		I sure was lucky that time.
		I should . . . .

You deserve good things.
I love you no matter what.
You can do it.
Let's find a solution.
You are worthwhile.
Let's play responsibly.
I'll teach you when you are
    ready.
May I tell you what I believe
    is in your best interest?
I accept your decision to feel
    unhappy.
I like it when you do that.
I need for you to . . . .
	**True
	Self**
		I deserve good things.
		I love me no matter what.
		I'm perfect.
		I can . . . .
		I choose to.
		I'm worthwhile.
		I need that.
		I keep my light at my feet.
		I deserve to feel good the
		    way I do.
		I do what is truly in my best
		    interest.
		I am happy or on my way.
		I like it when I do that.

We just can't wait any
    longer.
Let's play no matter what.
I love you because you
    take care of me.
I can't do without you.
You make me feel so good.
	Immature	I'm so lonely.
		I'm afraid.
		It's too hard to do.
		I'll do better later.
		I'm bored.
		All that matters is it feels so
		    good.
		I have to have it now.

I hate you. You make me feel bad. You made me do it. You aren't fair to me. I'll get even with you.	**Self**	I can't live without . . . . But I have to. I don't like it. It's not fair. I'll get even with her. I'm a bad person. I just know . . . .

marked off into three sections. See yourself moving to and sitting down in the middle of the center section.

You don't need to be limited to the images I've recommended. You can create images of your own that can work even better for you.

Stress and Mood Mastery Meditation

What we imagine in a meditative state can have a greater, more positive effect on us than ordinary imagining. In a meditative state we are able, in a sense, to fine tune our imagination for clearer "reception" by the subconscious.

Better reception isn't the only benefit. The positive and truthful messages we give ourselves can have a far greater effect.

Some benefits of Stress and Mood Mastery Meditation are: quick relief from upset, a feeling of well-being, sure escape from worry, greater confidence, calm without a loss of alertness, an ability to think more clearly, and real help to solve problems.

To practice what I call Stress and Mood Mastery Meditation, all you need is a quiet place, a few minutes, and a willingness to master your stress and moods. Start by sitting or lying down in a relatively quiet place. Then close your eyes.

Don't try to relax. A goal is to find out how effectively you can *rest*. If you happen to relax in the process, fine. If you don't, that's fine also.

Wait a minute. I thought the idea was to try to relax when you are having too much stress. There are even relaxation exercises for this. So what do you mean, telling me not to relax?

With relaxation, we too often get sleepy and unclear in our thinking. We don't want either of those about 80 percent of the time we're awake. We certainly don't want to be sleepy or have foggy thinking at work. Meditation allows us to be calm and still be alert.

The next step in Stress and Mood Mastery Meditation is: Focus your attention on where you are touching what's beneath you. Notice where your back touches, for example. If your mind wanders away, don't fuss at yourself. Bring your mind back to noticing where you touch and letting yourself rest more firmly. Find out how much you can trust what you are resting upon to support you. Allow your body to rest as firmly as you can.

Next, practice breathing in a restful way. Breathe in through your nose and out through your mouth. Let the air flow easily, without forcing it. As you let out the air, say the word *rest* to yourself. To the degree you can, picture yourself resting there, very deeply resting.

After you've rested a while, practice being in the here and now. Notice various bodily sensations such as warmth or coolness in your hands or face. If thoughts of the past or future slip in, shoo them away. You may be aware of different sounds or of quiet. Stay in the here and now as well as you can.

During meditation you can be aware of conditions such as heaviness in your arms or legs, easy breathing, and a lack of movement in your body. Maybe you'll notice a slight movement of your eyes beneath your closed eyelids. These are frequent signs of being in a meditative state.

When you believe you are in a meditative state, you can begin to use your imagination.

But what if I can't—"can't" thinking—I mean, what if I don't know if I'm in a meditative state?

The first few times you practice, you probably won't be sure. Spend a few minutes doing the resting and breathing, and say *rest* as you breathe out. Be in the here and now. Then, whether you can tell you're meditating or not, go on with the next part, to *imagine*. Think of yourself reliving situations you experienced before where you were not the master of your stress. Now (in your imagination) you are very much the master of how you feel and behave. You are free of needless anxiety, anger, or sadness.

In this meditative state, *you can say affirmations;* even more helpful, picture the words of the affirmations as you say them. "See" those words going down to the subconscious stream of thought and pushing negative, self-defeating thoughts far down, out of the way.

Before you end the meditation by opening your eyes, tell yourself that in the future whenever you take a deep breath and say "rest" as you breathe out, you will be able to recapture (in an instant) all of this calm but alert meditative state that you need.

Just Say "Quack"

As often as you catch yourself doing duck-like thinking, using duck dialogue terms, or feeling stress or upset, say the word *Quack* to yourself. You can say it to yourself or aloud. When possible, shout it out in your imagination (or do it for real, provided you can shout it comfortably and not disturb others).

Why do you want me to say *quack* when I'm thinking duck?

To make a powerful impression on the deeper part of your mind. It's as though you're saying to yourself, "Now pay attention to what you're thinking! I don't intend to put up with this duck-like false thinking that hurts me so much. So watch it!"

When I'm driving to the office and find myself feeling tense (stress), I'll shout out "Quack!" in the car. Often, just doing that's enough to calm me down. It's a short-hand version of saying to myself, "All right, you're thinking duck again—probably 'I just know' thinking. 'I just know that there's going to be a lot to do when I get to work.' So stop it!"

See with Eagle Eyes

The angry and bitter woman I was listening to was crying. "I don't want to work so hard ["it's too hard" thinking]. I have to [mind in the gotta] work on getting a better relationship with a man. I have to [mind in the gotta] work to feel better. It's so difficult ["it's too hard" thinking]." Whatever I told her she rebuffed. Before I could even complete my suggestions, she was telling me she had tried them before and they didn't help at all. In her opinion, I didn't understand her.

I could feel the usual signs of stress in me. The muscles between my shoulder blades were beginning to hurt. My stomach felt queasy and my hands were getting cool. No question, I was thinking pure duck.

What did I do? I looked at her with eagle eyes. I imagined that my eyes changed to those of a wonderful, soaring eagle. I left behind previous experiences of interacting with angry, crying women. I thought of how her upset and criticism weren't her; they were like dirty clothes covering her. I knew her anger was with herself, not with me. Then it became easy for me to be relaxed and to respond with compassion. If I'd become upset with her or defensive, I would've confirmed her poor opinion of herself.

Get ready for whatever will happen in your life by practicing seeing with eagle eyes. Look at a particularly unpleasant person, or a personality on television, who you thought used to get you stressed and upset. Only now look with your wonderful eagle eyes; see clearly what was difficult to make out before. The unpleasant person no longer has a negative influence on you. You see through his or her behavior to the lovable and worthy person beneath. Where you were tense before, you're now calm and caring.

Don't confine using your eagle eyes to viewing others. Look at yourself that way also. Practice while you're looking in a mirror.

How's seeing with eagle eyes different from how I usually do it?

You've probably had the experience of meeting for the first time someone who had been described to you by someone else and finding the new person a lot nicer than the other person had described. When that happens, you're seeing the new person with eagle eyes—you're observing from the here and now perspective. You see the person who is—not the person who has been. Your seeing is much more accurate.

Looking with duck eyes means your point of view is from the past. History is influencing you far more than is warranted. A man who, for example, views his wife's actions from the perspective of comparing them to how his mother did things is seeing with duck eyes. "Mom always ["always/never" thinking] had dinner ready by 6:30." A woman who treats her husband badly because he (or someone else, perhaps her father) has been a negative influence before, is using duck eyes. "You're just like ["always/never" thinking] my father."

But if someone has taken advantage of me before, shouldn't I take that into consideration and be careful?

You need to be watching out for any tendency you might have to allow others to ignore your important needs. That says more about how you feel about yourself than about your attitude toward others. As you know yourself better (see yourself more with eagle eyes) and like yourself better, there's little chance you'll feel others have treated you badly. Because you genuinely care about yourself, you'll protect yourself even better by constructive confrontation, when need be. "I'm not about to let the needs of a valuable person like me go unmet."

All right, I think I understand now.

An Additional Word

I've noticed over the years that people will sometimes find out about what they can do to master their stress and even agree it needs to be done, and then not do it. Or they begin but they don't stay with it long enough to do any good.

You are going to be perfect (perfectly you), worthwhile, important, and much more, whether you do what I recommend or not. You are going to be far more stressed, less happy, and less successful than you deserve if you don't practice stress mastery techniques long enough to help.

As much as I have a right to, I strongly encourage you to do what needs to be done and keep on doing it!

Change What You Eat and Drink

Because of the studying I've done and the books I've written dealing with good eating and exercise, I have come to realize that our menus most definitely influence our stress and moods. Menus high in stimulants like caffeine increase the likelihood of stress as well as anxious, fearful, or angry moods. Menus high in fat promote sluggish, low-energy (lazy) moods. If we eat or drink an excess of simple carbohydrates, such as those found in candy, sugary desserts, processed grains, and alcohol, we're more likely to be "down in the dumps" or depressed.

Is there anything left to eat and drink? It seems like everything I like is supposed to be bad for me.

There's plenty left. Only a small percentage of all foods and drinks hurtfully influence our level of stress and our moods. We still have plenty to choose from.

Foods and beverages that are high in protein, while not being high in dietary fat, give us greater alertness, clearer thinking (for stress mastery, that's extremely important), and more energy. Baked fish, chicken (cooked without the skin), skim milk, and low-fat cottage cheese are just some examples of such high-protein/low-fat foods.

Foods that are high in complex carbohydrates have a calming effect that helps reduce physical stress, fear, and anger. Vegetables, fruits, and whole grain cereals and breads are in this category.

Six keys to relieving stress and helping our mood with better eating and drinking are important. The first deals with alcohol.

I sometimes enjoy a drink, but I don't think I have a problem with it. I'm not an alcoholic.

There's an inventory in Chapter 10. If you have any doubts, you can use that inventory to find out what you need to know. Here now are the six points on stress and menus.

1. Unless alcohol is used only occasionally and without hurting our health, relationships, career, and responsible behavior, we need to show love for ourselves by avoiding alcohol completely. (Alcohol most definitely includes beer and wine.)

2. If we have trouble staying under one or maybe two "doses" of caffeine a day, then we deserve to treat ourselves well and eliminate it. (A dose of caffeine is a cup of coffee, a glass of tea, or a regular-sized can of soda.)

3. We should treat ourselves well by at least reducing our intake of high-fat foods such as red meat (unless used to flavor

vegetables), hard cheeses, whole milk, butter, margarine, oils (unless lightly sprayed), mayonnaise, nuts, and most salad dressings.

Young children, say four years or younger, may well need more fat than is recommended here. If you have any doubts at all, ask your pediatrician.

------

4. We can reward ourselves by all but eliminating processed sugar from our menus. Processed sugar is found in candy, sugary desserts, soft drinks, fruit juices (unless diluted with clean water), white (processed) breads, corn sweetener, syrup, dextrose, fructose, molasses, and honey (that's right: honey).
5. We deserve nothing less than to get our salt intake as low as we possibly can. Salt is tough on our bodies. It increases blood pressure and causes the retention of fluids, and these effects on our bodies negatively influence our stress and moods. We get naturally from foods that have no salt added the amount of salt we need, and we maintain it. There's no need for adding salt, ever.
6. Drink plenty of good, clean water. I recommend at least six large glasses of water per day in addition to the other beverages we drink. Water is definitely the drink of stress and mood masters.

Still, I'm not sure just how to do what you're recommending. It sounds like a drastic change.

Part of what you need is to have a different perspective where food and drink are concerned. That different perspective or point of view can make the needed changes far easier to accomplish. Chapter 8 gives some specifics.

Play Your Way to Less Stress and a Better Mood

I was watching an educational television program one evening and the commentator, talking about wildlife, said, "The more evolved an animal, the more likely it is going to play. It'll need to play." If we think of humans as being more evolved than animals, then our inclination toward and our need for play are far greater.

I used to think the more mature and intelligent a person is or the more technical and important the work he or she does, the less he or she wanted to and needed to play. Now I understand that, if anything, the opposite is true. Such people need to play even more. They may not want to at first, but they surely need it.

What do you call *play?*

Any activity that is looked forward to and usually enjoyed and that serves as a release or diversion from what one calls "work." While the activity of play may serve to improve ability or success at work, it is not thought of as being work. Play may or may not involve competition (I personally believe the most effective play doesn't involve competition) but does give a chance to feel a sense of accomplishment. Play can be done with others or alone and usually involves physical activity that is kept up more than just a few minutes. The less time we are willing (or tell ourselves we are able) to devote to play, the more vigorous it needs to be when we do it.

From what I've just said about play, you can probably get a good sense of what I believe are its biggest benefits. Still, I want to point out those benefits a bit more.

- Play invigorates the thinking process. We think more clearly as a result of playing. Vigorous physical activity, which is a part of most playing, helps to get more needed blood to our brain. We turn down our conscious thought processes during play and open up ourselves to creative ideas and insights from our subconscious stream of thought. (Some of the best solutions to life's problems come from that source.)

- Vigorous play, the kind I recommend the most, isn't only good for our brain. It's also good for our heart, lungs, and other vital organs. The better our bodies work, the easier it is to deal with excess and hurtful stress and be in a better mood.

- Play is usually fun and enjoyable. (Notice I said "usually." For example, running can definitely be play. However, experienced runners will tell you that the first ten minutes or so of a run is not much fun. It can be really uncomfortable and even hurt more than a bit. But as soon as the body warms up some and starts to adjust to the vigorous movement, it starts to be enjoyable.) The very important "child" part of the personality of every one of us wants and needs to have fun. To not play is to neglect that part, to be guilty of child neglect. So don't neglect your child.

- Play that's vigorous, such as walking, running, and aerobic dancing, helps to speed up our metabolism to get rid of excess body fat and gives more energy to do other things. Looking and feeling better then enhances how we feel about ourselves. There's little in life more important than our sense of self-esteem.

- As we become more skillful or accomplished at our play, that too can add to our positive self-image.

Physical play is so important to our stress mastery and improved moods, I'm devoting Chapter 9 to giving more details about it.

Other Components to Improve

If I continued to explore with you all the important things we can do for the sake of our stress and moods, this book would be way too long. Still, I want to mention a few additional points. Please understand that my brief attention to what follows doesn't at all say that they're unimportant.

- Sleep and rest give us the opportunity we require for "repairs" or physical recovery from work and play. Thinking eagle thoughts is easier when we're well rested.

- Involvement with family, friends, neighbors, and others increases our sense of being a part of a larger whole. It can comfort us, enhance our moods, and lessen stress by encouraging eagle thinking in us. Relationships can, in part, help validate and strengthen eagle thinking through support or opposition.

- Research has compared tranquilizers to sex as a means of relieving nervous tension and promoting sleep. It was reported that sex beat out the tranquilizers easily. So besides being fun, sex is good for our nerves and promotes the sleep needed for better moods.

- The more we learn what's true, the freer we are of excess stress. Our brain works better—we think more accurately—when exercised well or challenged with new things to learn. Continued study and learning are important all of our lives.

- "Mood music" is an expression sometimes used to describe music that can influence our moods and stress. My belief is that some music encourages positive thinking to come to the surface from our subconscious streams of thought; other music does just the opposite. Experimentation with different music can help us discover which does which. (Much popular music contains duck thinking, as in "The Way You Make Me Feel" and "I Can't Help It.")

- Look for humor and for what's positive in events that may appear tragic. One dark evening in May 1989 my wife, our cat L.A. (named for her large behind), and I huddled in the dark in what we judged to be the safest part of our home as tornado winds roared outside. L.A. meowed loudly, probably because she could hear sounds of great destruction that we couldn't hear. The next day our neighborhood looked as though a huge bomb had gone off. Few of the beautiful trees were left standing. (It really is true that the tallest trees catch the most wind.) There were literally layers of trees lying on top of layers of trees. In my yard alone, nearly 30 trees were down or damaged beyond saving. It was a miracle that no one was killed or seriously injured.

An anonymous neighbor who has a good sense of humor fashioned a sign and fastened it beneath the metal sign the city put up to announce to visitors that there was *no outlet* street in our neighborhood (you go out the way you go in). The homemade sign read "No Trees." Months later, the sign was still there, providing a needed chuckle to those of us who passed it daily.

I found that I began to focus on positives that came from the storm. My garden, which had far too much shade before, now had plenty of sunlight, essential to growing most vegetables and flowers. I also found that without the trees I could view sunrises and sunsets more easily than before.

Mission Possible

I want to finish this chapter with a discussion of creating and using a mission, a topic I feel very strongly about and I promised back in Chapter 3 I'd explain.

Few happenings influence us more negatively than thinking we're lost. Unless we know where we are and where we're going, we can have an ongoing, stress-producing sensation of being lost. And we can have it and not be usually aware of it.

Perhaps you sometimes have the sense of it as you wonder, "What's my life about?" "Does my life have real meaning?" "After I die, will people be able to tell and care that I was here?" "Am I going in the right direction?"

Remember when I was talking about walking the path and sometimes checking your compass?

Yes. You said something about using the compass to be sure of going in the direction I want to go.

The *compass* I am talking about is *your mission in life*. Checking it— clarifying and confirming your mission—can have a wonderfully soothing effect on you. I highly recommend it.

I've heard and read about people with missions. None of them seem like average people like me. I wonder if having a mission is something for me.

Please, consider the prospect that you and others don't identify such people as average *because they have a mission.* Having a mission is what causes them to be seen as extraordinary in other ways. You may mistakenly believe, "Only special people have something as special as a mission."

If you don't already have such a quest—a strong and consistent sense of purpose in your life—you very much need one to help relieve stress and build your secret self-esteem.

How do I go about getting a mission in my life?

First, you need to understand some characteristics of missions.

- A mission reflects your value. It isn't something you do, or have to try, to become valuable. You take the position, "I'm going in this direction because I am worthwhile."

- Because it reflects you, a mission is worthy. It's positive and makes a contribution to the well-being of others and you.

- You don't judge your mission in relation to others. You avoid thinking of it as better or worse than the mission of someone else. You don't compare. If it's yours, it's good enough.

- Accepting your mission as it is doesn't mean it doesn't change. It usually does change and grow or evolve over time. It might start out complex and become increasingly simple. Or it could do just the opposite: start simple and become complex.

- A mission doesn't often change completely but it can. Don't feel that when you determine what your mission is you have to stick with it always. You have a right to change the direction of your path.

- Missions don't interfere with the rights or needs of others or attempt to control them. You would successfully avoid, for example, a mission to try and influence someone to live a life (make choices) that you didn't, but wish that you had. A mother's unacceptable mission might be to try to get her daughter to be the actress she wasn't.

- You need to write down and think about your mission. This is particularly important. Just as with a compass, you regularly take your mission out and examine it. A compass or a mission left in your pocket is worthless.

Let me finish this description with an example of a mission that started out simple and became more complex with time. It was worthy, and reflected the value (worth) of its owner.

The first time the mission was written, it was:	"Help people."
Several weeks later it became:	"Help people the best I can."
After changing gradually over the years, it now reads:	"Help others and myself as well and as long as I can in ways and places I enjoy. The help I offer is the chance to enhance mental and physical well-being."

The mission you come up with doesn't need to be stated in terms of helping. It can be whatever suits you. Write a mission that you sense is going in the right direction. Occasionally take it out and read it. If you feel the need, rewrite it.

Having a mission relieves stress and builds self-esteem, but it also does something more: your mission becomes a major, positive force in your life. You'll find yourself doing things that later turn out as serving your mission when you didn't know that would happen. Your awareness grows. You see opportunities you didn't recognize before.

Foods to Master Stress and Moods

The Foods That Will Help with the Stress That Gets Past Your Eagle Thinking

By thoughtfully evaluating and, if necessary, changing what you eat and drink, you can help yourself in many ways:

- Some foods and drinks, especially those with sugar and alcohol, encourage the thinking that leads to increased depression, anger, and fearfulness. Using less or little of those foods, you can stay in better spirits.
- You can avoid adding weight (fat). Being fat is definitely a negative influence on stress and mood.
- Certain foods and drinks encourage the use of nicotine or other addictive drugs. By purposefully using less of those foods, you help yourself.
- You feel more like exercising when you're eating and drinking well.

As long as we insist on consuming foods and drinks that damage us, we are going to hurt. The damage for many people will be considerable stress, painful emotions, and excess fat. The hurt for some will also be diseases such as cancer and heart disease.

I tell people, and I'm serious, "If you think it really matters what foods and drinks you love or like to eat, you're making an honest mistake. What truly matters is, what foods and drinks like and love *you?* You deserve the liking and loving, not the food and drink."

As I think more of me, I think less of food and drink.

These insights about foods and drinks help to explain why I sometimes refer to them in terms of which ones love us, like us, are indifferent, dislike, or hate us. The foods and drinks that love us the most are the lowest in salt, sugar, and fat and relatively high in dietary fiber. They help us to avoid becoming stressed, fat, fearful, angry, depressed, and subject to addictions and diseases.

Foods and drinks are really fuel, not medications, entertainment, or works of art. Keeping to this basic concept, I've created a "fuel list" that appears in the next few sections. If you don't find a particular food or group of foods on the list, you are safer to assume that consuming it is hurtful.

Foods That Are Best

Water

Water from the tap, or bottled spring water, or seltzer is essential for you. An adult typically needs at least six or seven large glasses of water a day, aside from any other liquid intake. Plenty of water is particularly essential when you're consuming the amount of dietary fiber your body deserves. Water helps to reduce constipation and fluid retention, and can help you to avoid stomach trouble and adding fat.

Vegetables

Eat vegetables raw, baked, boiled, steamed, or stir-fried in water or a small amount of vegetable oil. Use them to make delicious soups. Canned vegetables packed in water with no salt have the least nutrition; frozen vegetables have higher food value, but fresh vegetables are best. Those with deep colorings are excellent. Sprouts and most legumes (peas, beans, and lentils) are considered vegetables.

Whole Grains

Breads, cereals, pasta, and corn and rice with the bran still in them are whole-grain foods. They need to be as low in salt, oil, and processed sugar (honey, powdered or granular sugar, or corn sweetener) as possible. Breads that are whole grain are labeled 100 percent whole wheat or rye.

Skim Milk

Milk is an important source of calcium, and milk low in fat is the best source. Skim milk has one percent or less fat, whether you buy it as a liquid or as a powder to be mixed with water. One or two glasses a day, "straight" or mixed with grains or fruit, are recommended. Skimmed plain yogurt, uncreamed or "dry" cottage cheese (also called pot cheese or farmers' cheese), and grated parmesan cheese are in the skim-milk category.

Foods that are best for you promote relaxation.

Fruit in Good Company

Fresh fruits or fruits packed in their own juice give beneficial flavoring to other foods, such as whole grains. Cantaloupe (musk melon), strawberries, apples, and bananas are four of the best mixers.

Juice in Water

Juices are good flavorings for a glass of water. One of my favorite drinks is apple fizz: cold seltzer water and just enough pure apple juice to flavor it.

A client who was getting free of smoking reported to me some time back that he was doing well but he was having some stomach discomfort. His withdrawal from nicotine (tobacco) sometimes gave him a "gnawing" feeling in his stomach. He tried to remedy it by eating or drinking.

He knew enough to stay away from foods high in sugar and fat. When I heard he was eating fruit and drinking fruit juices, I suspected they were causing part of the stomach trouble. I suggested that he reduce his intake of juice by mixing it with water—maybe cold seltzer water. I recommended that small amounts of baked white or sweet potato, with no added fat or margarine, be substituted for some of the fruit. He did as I suggested, and later reported that it worked out well.

Egg Whites (Cooked)

Many recipes work as well using only egg whites instead of whole eggs. Egg whites are cholesterol-free.

Foods That Are Good

Vegetable Juices

Fresh vegetable juices are recommended over canned vegetable juices, which usually have too much added salt. Some low-salt varieties are available, especially in health-food stores.

High-protein foods promote energy and alertness.

White Meats and Fish

These include most fresh fish, rabbit, chicken, and turkey breast. White meats are at their very best when cooked free of the skin by any method but frying or when mixed with fresh vegetables. Cold-water fish such as salmon and mackerel are preferred. Canned fish that's water-packed and drained has marginal value.

Catsup, Mustard, Vinegar, and Tomato Sauces

Make your own or look for varieties low in salt, processed sugars, and oils.

Fruits

Choose any fruit. Fresh fruit is free of added sugar.

Low-Fat Dairy Products

These include low-fat milk, low-fat yogurt, low-fat cottage cheese, and regular buttermilk.

Foods That Are Typically Indifferent

Artificial Sweeteners

Equal is the most well known form of aspertame. Some people are allergic to it, but, for most of us, it's evidently harmless. Sweet One, another low-calorie sweetener, has the advantage of staying sweet when heated.

Egg Substitutes

These have little or no fat and cholesterol, but may have too much salt for those who need to keep their intake of salt as low as possible. Make sure you read the labels carefully.

Butter Substitutes

Butter Buds and Molly McButter are fat-free, but have salt you may need to avoid.

Dried Fruit, Fruit Spreads, and Juice Concentrates

These are fine when added to whole grains as flavoring, but they need to be free of extra sugar.

Salt Substitutes

These are stepping stones toward a salt-free diet. Eventually, it's best to avoid even the salt substitutes.

Diet Soda

Look for those that are free of sugar and caffeine and are also low in salt (35 mg or less).

Shellfish

Shrimp, scallops, lobster, crabs, oysters, clams, mussels, and crawfish are in this category.

Decaffeinated Coffee and Tea

If you use decaffeinated coffee, use one that has had the caffeine removed through a water process, such as Sanka. Lipton makes a good decaffeinated tea.

Red and Dark Meats

Cuts of beef (U.S.D.A. "good" rather than "choice" or "prime" grade), veal, pork, and lamb, in small amounts and trimmed free of most of the fat, can be added to vegetables, soups, or casseroles as a flavoring. The same can be done with the dark meat of chicken or turkey, cooked without the skin, which contains fat and cholesterol.

When I talk with people about eating less red meat, I occasionally hear, "But I don't care for [don't-like thinking] chicken and fish that much. And here you are telling me I shouldn't [oughty thought] eat my steaks."

I tell them I'm offering guidelines regarding red meat and other foods. "I don't have the 'grate expectation' of you that you will do what's ideal. If you're finding it hard to follow these food and drink guidelines, I'd recommend you focus more on building how you feel about yourself, down deep. Your choice of foods and drinks will change, if need be, in response to your stronger secret self-esteem."

Whole Eggs

Whole eggs don't benefit those of us who have a problem with cholesterol. For the rest of us, whole eggs are likely to be all right when combined in recipes, in reasonable amounts. Whenever possible, add less whole egg than a recipe calls for. If a recipe calls for two eggs, put in the whites of both eggs and the yolk of only one of them.

Foods That Are Bad

Dried Fruits Alone

When eaten by themselves, dried fruits can be bad, since they contain too much concentrated sugar.

Undiluted Fruit Juices

When undiluted, there's often excessive sugar and acid in fruit juices.

Processed Grains

These have little benefit without the bran part of the grain. White breads and light brown breads (those with only some whole grains) are made from processed grains.

Saccharin

There's evidence that saccharin can harm us.

Salt (Sodium)

Salt harms us when added to foods during or after cooking or when added to drinks. Extra salt is particularly hurtful when we have excess stress. Salt tends to negatively influence blood pressure; stress raises blood pressure too.

Whole Eggs (Main or Side Dishes)
Eat fewer yolks. They're high in fat and cholesterol.

Foods That Are Most Harmful for You

Caffeine
This stimulant–drug, found in cola drinks, cocoa, tea, and coffee, is particularly harmful to those who suffer with hypertension, excess stress, and ulcers. Pregnant or nursing women need to consult with their physicians about its use. Caffeine is addictive.

Reducing Caffeine

- Switch to hot or iced decaffeinated tea.
- Drink only decaffeinated soft drinks.
- If you drink more than one cup of coffee, switch to decaffeinated after the first cup.
- Buy coffee with and without caffeine. When you make coffee, mix the two. Over time, add more and more of the decaffeinated and less of the coffee with caffeine.

Fatty Foods
All untrimmed and fatty (lower than 75 percent lean) cuts of red meats, such as ribs and chops; whole milk, margarine, butter, and most cheeses; oils, coconut, nuts and peanut butter, seeds, and wheat germ; olives and avocados—all are fatty foods.

Reducing Fat in Foods

- Prepare soups and stews ahead, then chill and scrape off the hardened fat.
- Remove the skin from poultry before cooking.

- Trim most of the fat from meats.
- Drain off fat whenever possible.
- Use non-stick pans or a little vegetable oil spray.
- Stir-fry with water or a little oil.
- Bake, broil, poach, and boil foods instead of frying.
- Replace oils in marinades with other liquids such as vegetable broth.

Processed Sugars

These include granular and powdered sugar (white or brown), honey, molasses, syrup, corn sweetener, processed fructose, dextrose, and glucose added to food and drink. Processed sugar gives something of a lift in energy at first. Later, energy declines and depression or irritability is common.

Get Free of Processed Sugar

When I went "cold turkey" off processed sugar, I'd get strong cravings. At first I'd want something very sweet and it seemed that only sugar would do. After a while the cravings got strong enough that anything sweet, not just refined sugar and chocolate, would suffice. That's when I hit upon the idea of eating pitted dates until the cravings subsided. The dates, by themselves, weren't good for me but they were a step in the right direction. After a while, I was satisfied with a couple of chopped dates on some whole-grain cereal. Somewhere along the way, I got rid of my taste for dates. There's no way that would have ever happened with processed sugar or chocolate. Note: If you use pitted dates, still watch out for pits.

Nicotine

While not usually thought of as a food, nicotine is taken in by mouth and is similar to caffeine. Like caffeine, nicotine is a drug and a stimulant. It is also highly addictive and poisonous.

Get Free of Smoking

The following is too simple to help many people who are addicted to nicotine. Even so, use it and see how far you can get. You might surprise yourself.

Make an I Choose Life List by writing the words "I choose life" at the top of an index card. Then write two or more *positive* reasons for not smoking at all. When you want to smoke, read the card. As often as you can think of it, put the stem of a whole clove in your mouth. (Clove is the spice that's stuck in hams to season them as they cook. Take care not to inhale the stem into your lung.) Keep the clove in your mouth until any urge to smoke goes away. You can use this to gradually reduce your smoking or go "cold turkey."

Alcohol

This drug is also addictive, and its effects can be extremely harmful. It's amazing how many people who drink beer and wine don't think they are using alcohol. Beer and wine have the same kind of alcohol that whiskey drinkers use. Studies that have reported alcohol to be helpful "used in moderation" may be saying much more about the people who are able to use it that way than about the substance itself. Alcohol is fine when cooked. The heat evaporates the alcohol and leaves the flavor.

Reducing Alcohol

Using less of the depressing and addictive drug called alcohol can be a real problem. Though used somewhat less than in previous years, alcohol is still well entrenched as a social "lubricant." If you suspect you're addicted to alcohol, the only sure way to deal with it is to be *entirely* free of it. For those who are profoundly addicted, getting and staying free of alcohol is a challenge beyond the scope of this book. But for others, there are two recipes for drinks that can help in getting and staying free of alcohol. They look and taste somewhat like alcoholic drinks, without being alcoholic.

PILOT'S COCKTAIL

Sparkling water, seltzer, or soda   A squeeze of fresh lime or lemon
  water

Dash of angostura bitters

Mix and serve over ice. Note: Ingredients are readily available in any
well stocked bar.

COLD BUT CARING JUICE FIZZ

Cold bottled seltzer water (or   Grape juice or other juice that
  sparkling water)   you prefer, with no sugar
                                           added.

Add the juice to cold seltzer water, to taste. Serve as is or over ice.

Last Notes about the Food List

You can take a good vitamin/mineral supplement (not high or
megadose amounts) recommended by your physician or pharma-
cist. Younger women may need added iron, for example.

The food list is not a diet and doesn't replace a way of eating
prescribed by your physician, dietician, or nutritionist. If you have
any question about its value to you, ask your physician. It's hard to
imagine this information would be anything but helpful to anyone
over the age of four, but you are too important to take even the
slightest chance.

Reading Labels

In response to a growing awareness of food values on the part of
consumers, some food companies have gotten "creative." They put
statements on packages such as "100% natural," "all natural," "no
preservatives added." What they don't say is what those "natural"
or "non-preservative" ingredients are, in a way that can be easily
identified. They could be salt, sugar, oil, or other stuff that can
harm us.

You may think, as I did, the easy solution is to read labels. It
does help, but even that can be tricky unless you know the other
words that essentially mean the same as *salt* and *sugar.* Monosodium

glutamate, sodium phosphate, sodium nitrate, baking soda, and baking powder all add to the salt content of a product. Dextrose, glucose, fructose, corn syrup, corn sweetener, molasses, honey, and brown sugar are all different forms of sugar.

Remember that the ingredients of a product are listed in the order of how much of each is present. What a product has the most of goes first and the ingredient it has the least of is last. With some products, it's nearly impossible to avoid at least a little sugar. To get the least amount possible, compare labels and get the one that has sugar (whatever they call it) listed nearer to the end of the list of ingredients.

Eating Out

More places these days have salad bars—even some burger, steak, taco, and pizza restaurants. Those are the places I usually head for at mealtime. When I'm with others and we're deciding on somewhere to eat, I know I'm worth letting others know that I need a restaurant with a decent salad bar.

My specialty is a salad with wine vinegar as dressing and a baked potato. I order a plain potato, without anything on it that would be a bad influence. Often whoever is waiting on me will say, "You want it plain with just butter on it, right?" When I say that I want it free of everything, I sometimes get a strange look.

Salad bars don't exclusively offer foods that help to relieve and avoid stress. Some salad ingredients are high in oils and sugar, such as salad dressings, potato or macaroni salads, potato skins, and marinated vegetables.

If I'm not familiar with a salad bar, I'll ask if preservatives have been used on the vegetables. Chemical preservatives can change the most useful food into something quite different.

If I'm particularly hungry and I know I'm going to a place where it may be more of a challenge to get what I deserve, I eat something before I go, to dampen my appetite and give me the edge I need. At times like these a "cereal survival pack" comes in handy. The survival pack consists of some dry cereal (I prefer Grape Nuts), dry milk, raisins, and a plastic spoon in a zipper-type plastic bag. When I'm ready to eat, I add a little cold water to the contents (still in the bag) and I'm all set.

Avoid being negatively influenced by those you're eating with. Misery loves company. If they're eating and drinking what hurts and is bad for them, they'll want you to do it too. You'll hear statements such as, "This is such a nice restaurant. You don't want to miss out on all the goodies, do you?"

Remember that special places and special times make it even more important to treat yourself special.

9

Play Your Excess Stress Away

Exercises That Help Take
Care of the Stress That Slips By

Whether you enjoy vigorous physical play (exercise) regularly or occasionally, you're already on your way to needed relief. If you're not exercising, you have much to gain from starting. Here's just some of what's in it for you.

- Exercise, done the way that's suggested here, helps to relieve the stress that gets past even your best efforts to avoid it with eagle thinking. Vigorous exercise, for instance, eases muscle tension. And muscle tension is a part of physical stress.

- Vigorous exercise that's playful does wonders to decrease the inaccurate thinking that causes dangerous stress and moods. Playing and thinking negatively don't mix well at all.

- Even more than by changing what you eat and drink, you reduce the likelihood of adding fat. Exercise lessens your appetite while it speeds up your metabolism.

- Vigorous exercise is a positive replacement for what people get from a drug such as nicotine: a reduction in tension

173

followed by a lift in energy. Exercise makes it easier to stay away from tranquilizing drugs and stimulants.

Did you notice I said "vigorous exercise" instead of only saying "exercise"?

Yes, I did. How come?

For exercise to be helpful in the ways you want and you deserve, it needs to be vigorous enough to raise your pulse rate significantly and keep it up for several minutes at a time.

When I say "vigorous," I don't mean unpleasant, unsafe, or painful. I decided years ago that I needed a new word that said more clearly what I meant, so I created the word *PlayRobics*. We'll talk more about that shortly.

Physical Activity That Helps

The kind of physical activity that's essential, to get and keep a safe level of stress and better moods, is *aerobic* activity. Aerobic means "air-using" or "with air." It encourages you to use larger amounts of air. To do that, you need to get your pulse up to between 100 and 160 beats per minute and then keep it there for at least 20 minutes at a time. With non-aerobic exercise, I'd get my pulse up to well over 100 beats per minute—perhaps using weight-lifting machines or playing ball—and it would soon drop to below 100. That took away most of the benefit I was wanting out of the exercise.

Are there any precautions I need to take?

As a rule, the less experienced we are with exercise, the older we are, or the poorer our physical condition, the more we need to keep our pulse rate down near 100. At least start at or near 100 and over a period of weeks increase it, if you need to and can do it safely. Anyone with a heart condition or a family history of heart disease needs to undertake this kind of physical activity only with the advice and monitoring of a physician.

To take your pulse, feel just beside your "Adam's apple" on your throat. Press just firmly enough to feel your pulse. (If you press too hard you can get a false reading.) As you feel your pulse with your fingertips, count the beats for six seconds and multiply the count by 10 to get your pulse rate for one minute. Let's say that you take your pulse at your neck for six seconds (one-tenth of a minute) and have counted 12 beats. You would multiply 12 by 10, or simply add a zero to the twelve, for a total of 120. That means that 120 was your pulse rate for a minute.

Be sure to take your pulse every few minutes during aerobic activity, to keep an accurate track of it. I recommend taking it every three or four minutes during the first few weeks. When you're more experienced, you'll be able to take it less often and still do very well keeping it where it needs to be.

Your Exercise Speedometer

Think of some people you love dearly and pretend they're just beginning to drive a car. You'd like them to get where they want to go on time, but you want them to get there safely, right?

Would you want them to ride with their speedometer taped up so they couldn't see it?

Of course not. Without being able to look at the speedometer, chances are they'd either go too slow to get where they want to go on time, or they would go too fast and be unsafe.

The same is true if you exercise without taking your pulse regularly. Your pulse rate is your *exercise speedometer*. Unless you're using it, you may be going "too slow" to get where you want and need to be. You won't get there on time. If you're going "too fast," you're unsafe and are creating more problems than you're solving.

If it's so important to take your pulse when you exercise, how come I hardly ever see anyone who's exercising doing it?

Partly, for the same reason that duck-like thinking survives from one generation to the next. Those who are learning to exercise learn from those who have learned wrong. Misinformation simply gets passed along. Also, some people who're exercising may be using an "exercise speedometer" that's not obvious, like the one that follows.

Another way of keeping track of how well you're treating yourself and getting your heart rate up to where it needs to be is to follow the *"conversation rule."* If you engage in an aerobic activity and you can easily carry on a conversation, you're probably not doing enough; your pulse isn't between 100 and 160. You need to put out more energy. If you aren't able to carry on a conversation, you're doing too much and need to ease off a bit. The ideal is to be able to carry on a conversation, but with some effort. You can easily tell you are breathing harder, but you aren't uncomfortable or out of breath.

Important: After 20 to 60 minutes of your aerobic activity, rest and cool down for five minutes. Then take your pulse again. If your pulse is still 100 or more, that's a sign that you were doing too much and need to take it easier the next time.

How Often to Do Aerobic Activity

How often do I need to do this exercise?

Doing it fewer than three times a week will probably bring too little benefit. It's best to gradually increase your aerobic activity to three to five times a week.

What about exercising six or more times a week?

Some people follow the "more is always better" philosophy: they figure that if doing something four or five times a week is great, then doing it six, seven, or even eight times a week will be even better. That isn't the case here. By increasing your activity much more than five times a week, you're running the risk of experiencing "exercise burnout." That means you can get too much of even the very best thing. It can become more a chore than the fun it needs to be.

PlayRobics

Exercise that works to help you be and stay free of dangerous stress and hurtful moods is like the play of childhood. It's fun, requires no companions or teachers, is safe, and takes little skill.

It is so different from what most consider to be "exercise," that I needed to call it something else. It deserved a new and better name, so I called it *PlayRobics*.

- PlayRobics responds to what I suspect is an inborn and powerful need for play.
- PlayRobics comes as close to being free from danger of physical injury as you can get.
- People who cannot safely do other exercise or aerobics can do PlayRobics.
- PlayRobics is habit-forming. It encourages in us a positive dependence in that it promotes a desire or craving to do it on a regular basis.
- It doesn't require the involvement of others. It promotes self-sufficiency rather than dependency.

Warming Up and Warming Down

Think about how you drive when you're going some distance from home. As you leave your immediate neighborhood, you drive slowly and carefully, maybe 10 or 15 miles per hour. You pick up your speed to around 30 or 35 miles per hour as you reach a secondary road. It isn't until you get to the highway that you increase to a speed that easily gets you somewhere. When you're returning home, you reverse what I just described. You slow down to perhaps 35 miles per hour and then to 10 or 15 miles per hour before you stop in your driveway.

It's easy to realize the importance of driving this way. You and others are much safer. Also, it's a lot easier on your car to increase and decrease speed gradually.

Our bodies deserve a great deal more care than our cars. When we do aerobic exercise, it's important to move gradually into (warm up) and move gradually out of (warm down) the activity.

Often, as I warm up and warm down from a PlayRobic activity, I'll mentally picture a speedometer. As I gradually increase the energy I put into the PlayRobic, I imagine the needle of the speedometer moving up. The same is done in reverse as I warm down and decrease my energy output.

How do I decide how much time to spend warming up and warming down?

How much time you put into it depends on how much experience you have with the activity. Another factor is how likely you are to be hurt. For example, running is great exercise, but it's an aerobic activity that can easily cause injured knees or feet because of the twisting motion of our bodies and the jarring effect of our feet hitting the hard surface beneath us. On the other hand, walking involves a much more natural motion of our bodies and there's little jarring involved. Walking and rebounding, using a small, trampoline-like device to exercise, are PlayRobic activities that make it easier to treat ourselves lovingly and avoid injury.

If you're not yet in good physical condition or using exercise like running, you need to spend more time warming up and warming down. I consider five minutes each to be the minimum amount of time needed for warm-up and warm-down, no matter what aerobic activity you're engaged in. If you're doing something such as running, you may need more.

Controlling Your Pulse Rate

Controlling your pulse rate, whether that means moving it up or down or keeping it steady, is crucial. When you begin an activity, it's largely time that increases your pulse rate. During the first few minutes, your pulse rate steadily increases; then it levels off. Soon after you stop exercising, your pulse decreases and levels off at your "resting pulse rate."

But let's say that you're using your favorite PlayRobic activity and after a while your pulse rate levels off at 100 beats per minute and you want it to be at least 120. In fact, you'd prefer that it be around 130. You are well warmed up, and you want to get your pulse rate up soon. What can you do?

One thing I could do is speed up—go faster.

Actually, there're three ways of increasing your pulse rate: First, you can speed up, as you said; making your muscles work faster will increase your pulse rate.

The second option is to get more muscles involved. Let's say you're walking and barely using your arms. You can keep the same speed but use your arms more, by swinging them. Your pulse rate will increase and again level off at a higher rate.

The third way to increase your pulse is to weight-load: add to the weight your muscles work against. Again, let's say you're walking and you want to increase your pulse to 130. You can keep the same speed, use no more muscle, but add weights to your body, and your pulse rate will increase. The weight you add could take one of many forms: a daypack you carry on your back, with bags of sand in it; weights that you strap to your ankles or wrists; small dumbbells that you carry in your hands; heavier shoes or boots.

If you find that your pulse is higher than is in your best interest —maybe you're shooting for 130 and find that your pulse is 150— you can reduce your pulse rate by doing the opposite of what it takes to increase it. You can reduce your speed, use fewer muscles, or reduce the weight your body is working against.

Important: Avoid reducing your pulse rate by suddenly stopping. Slow down, but keep going. Simply stopping is too tough on your body. Also, avoid taking a hot bath or shower soon after strenuous physical activity. It can cause your blood pressure to rise too high.

Safety and effectiveness are the most obvious reasons for knowing how to increase and decrease your pulse rate. There's another reason, too.

Some experts say, "Walking is okay for a beginner, but after a while, walking just won't be enough. The person exercising will need to begin a more vigorous exercise, such as running." Other experts are critical of rebounding because, they say, the springiness of the rebounder makes it too easy except for those who are very overweight or extremely out of shape. They conclude, "Rebound exercise has only very limited applications."

The reality is that by the thoughtful use of speed, muscle involvement, and weight loading, PlayRobics activities such as walking and rebounding are as effective and challenging as any other aerobic exercise. There may be some differences, however. Walking and rebounding may well be reliably more fun, require less skill, be more convenient, be less expensive, and be far less likely to lead to injury than most other aerobic exercises.

Let's examine some aerobic exercises.

Rebounding

I own two rebounders and regularly bounce on them. These are very small versions of trampolines and are many times safer than the large ones.

The typical rebounder is about three feet wide. It's usually round, but can be square. It stands on four or six legs, with the platform about eight inches off the floor. The surface is made of a strong, woven mat attached to a metal frame by heavy-duty steel springs. The frame and springs are covered by a foam-rubber pad and imitation leather. The tough and durable matting material resembles the stuff used for bulletproof vests.

Rebounding is gentle on joints and muscles, and it can be done indoors. Rebounding is so much fun that many people have continued to do it long after they would have given up on activities such as jogging and swimming. It strengthens many muscles of the body, including the most important muscle of all: the heart. It improves lung functioning. The benefit that interests many people is that rebounding helps to get free of excess fat nearly as effectively as jogging.

In recent years, I've kept a rebounder handy at the office. When I find I have duck-thought my way into being tense and tired, I bounce on the rebounder for three or four minutes to relieve the stress and give me an energy boost.

Give your rebounder your vigorous attention three to five times a week for 20 to 60 minutes each time. In return, rebounding will gently bathe you in warm mineral water (sweat) and lovingly help to get rid of excess stress, hurtful moods, and excess fat.

You deserve nothing less.

Stationary Bicycling

There are probably many millions of stationary bicycles gathering dust in attics and basements.

Why is it that stationary bikes are bought and not used that much?

Because most break easily, are extremely boring, or simply don't help toward exercise goals.

But you include them in your list of the better aerobic exercises.

Bicycles that are durable and work extremely well provide a safe, gentle, and complete aerobic conditioning. They're tremendous aids to getting free of and avoiding excess stress and painful moods, and developing physical well-being.

The catch is that most stationary bikes that work well are expensive (several hundreds of dollars). Probably the most well known is the Schwinn fan-type stationary bike. The last time I checked, its cost was about $600.

The Schwinn Fan-Type Bike

Part of what makes this stationary bike such a valuable machine is that it's durable and involves both the arms and legs in turning the wheel, which gets its resistance from metal fans that catch air as they move. You can easily control your pulse rate by pulling the

handle bars and pedaling faster or slower. The more energy you put into it, the more effectively it warms and works your body.

While it would be difficult to find an exercise bike that does a better job, this one is a bit noisy. It gives plenty of loving attention to your upper body, because of the pulling and pushing on the handlebars. Some people have needlessly given up on the fan-type bike because they went at it too hard at first. They needed to take it easier, to pedal and move the handlebars more slowly to conserve energy.

One alternative to buying a Schwinn fan-type bike is to join a health club or gym that has them available to members. Still another option is to check into leasing one, with what you pay in rent going toward payment if you later decide to buy it. That can give you a good chance to find out if you like it, without buying it first.

Improve Your Stationary Bike

If you already have a stationary bike that isn't that great, you can improve it. While you pedal, you can use arm movements, lifting light dumbbells or weights strapped to your wrists. Set the resistance to the pedals fairly easy and go to it.

By using arm movements with or without added weights as you pedal, you can add more fun and benefit to your bike. Even an inexpensive bike can be made much more helpful.

A woman in one of my seminars told me she couldn't use her exercise bike because it hurt her legs. When it was assembled her husband set the resistance on the bike to what he thought would be best for her. The resistance was so great that she could barely turn the pedals, and her legs hurt. I suggested that she adjust the resistance herself by lowering it until the pedals turned so easily that she could comfortably continue for quite a long time. Then she could check her pulse in four or five minutes to see if it was at the desirable level. If it was, she could leave the resistance alone. If not, she could increase the resistance a little and check her pulse again in four or five minutes. She could continue doing that until she found the resistance that was right for her.

Another problem people have with stationary bikes is that the seats are too low, and pedaling hurts their knees. The seat needs to be adjusted so your leg *almost straightens out* on the down stroke. But the seat needs to be low enough that you don't roll from side to side as you pedal.

Part of the benefit of the exercise bike is that you can ride in the comfort and privacy of your home while listening to music, watching television, or even reading. Exercise bikes give you good support and take the pressure off your back, hips, knees, and ankles.

The Computer-Type Stationary Bicycle

The computer-type bike has a simple computer and computer program inside it. Its display screen can be easily seen and has special graphics. As you begin to pedal, you choose how long you want to exercise and the top level of how hard you want to pedal. The computer program then simulates a ride outdoors on both level areas and hills.

This bike is more expensive than some others but may well be worth the cost. The special computer program is simple to use and the graphics make it interesting and easy to stick with. One of its few drawbacks is that it doesn't give you the chance to exercise your upper body as you pedal.

Bicycling

In case you've forgotten, ask any child about riding a bike and you'll be eagerly reminded how much fun it is; it's play. A bike allows you to cover a greater distance than running but at a speed that's still slow enough to enjoy your surroundings.

There are several advantages to riding a bike. It's gentle on your body. There's less jarring. And it's a pleasant motion that places little strain that's likely to injure joints or muscles. Biking is an exercise that can be enjoyed by young and old and most ages in between. You can involve the family in the activity. Many communities have set areas for bike riding. The expense is modest and the upkeep is minimal. Last, but far from least, bike riding can very effectively raise and keep the PlayRobic pulse rate that will help you to keep excess fat, duckish moods, and excess stress away.

There are also some disadvantages. Monitoring your pulse while riding a bike is difficult; you need to stop on a regular basis to do that. At the speeds necessary to get your pulse where it needs to be, there is more likelihood of falling, so be careful. In some areas, it may be necessary to stop and start a lot, which can make it more difficult to raise and keep your pulse up and is a general nuisance. There is a temptation to coast rather than continuing to pedal most of the time, as you need to. You're more limited in the times you can exercise, when you ride a bike. Wet surfaces and darkness can be hazardous. Good balance and skill are more important than in some other exercises that are as effective.

A good bike for those who've smoked, have significant excess fat or stress, or haven't biked in a while is one that has the wider "balloon" tires. Its handlebars don't require you to bend way over to ride and it doesn't have many gears. Unless you live in an area with lots of hills, you don't need many gears.

Since I live where there are many hills and I love to play on a bike, I bought a "mountain bike," a particularly rugged bike with fat tires, lots of gears (that are truly easy to use), and reliable hand brakes. It travels on trails about as well as on the road. I have great fun taking the mountain bike to the coast and riding on the beach. I can get down on the hard sand and ride "forever." If you do that, be sure to wash the bike after riding to keep it from rusting.

Where do you recommend getting a bike?

At a reputable bike shop, a store that specializes in selling bikes. The salesperson can help you to make sure you get a bike suited to your needs and your size. Don't let anyone talk you into an expensive racing or touring bike you'll rarely use. It's best to get one that's sturdy, balances easily, and is simple to ride.

At most shops, you can get a bike that you'll enjoy for under $300. I paid more for my mountain bike, but I've ridden enough years to know I'll definitely get my money out of it. The cheaper bikes sold in department stores typically won't operate as well or last as long. A bike-shop bike priced between $200 and $300 probably will. You're worth the investment and a great deal more.

Stair Climbing Machine

A while back, I "confessed" to Judy that I had "fallen in love" at the sports club. What I fell for was a stair climbing machine, a machine that simulates the act of climbing stairs. It's electric and has a computer and computer program in it. Like the computer-type stationary bicycle, the stair machine has a display you can watch that tells you how far you've gone in the exercise and how hard you're playing.

When you first use the stair machine, you can put it on the "manual" setting so you can increase and decrease the intensity of your play at will. Or you can select from a variety of special programs already in the computer. I suggest that you start with the "manual" function only. Start at a rate that you can do for a while, one that's too easy. Then gradually and safely increase the rate your legs need to move to keep up with the machine. Do this the first several times you use the machine. You don't need to try and keep up with others who've used the machine longer, or are using it incorrectly.

To get the most benefit, you need to *stand erect* and *avoid supporting your weight on your hands.* Just hold on to the rails firmly enough to be secure. Let your *feet go up and down nearly the complete*

range of motion, but *without the step hitting the top or the bottom.* Bending way over when you use the machine is what I call the "duck droop."

The down side of this apparatus is that (1) it easily allows cheating, and (2) it looks more difficult than it is. I regularly see people cheating on the machine by bending way over, supporting themselves too much with their arms, and taking tiny steps. This allows them to go at a higher pace without putting in a corresponding amount of energy. By making the small steps, rather than letting the step go nearly the full range of motion, they're also putting too much strain on their knees and working a too-small portion of their leg muscles.

Some people at the sports club stare at the stair machine and look as if they'd like to try it. My guess is that they mistakenly think it's difficult to learn to do, because of the computer part of it. Maybe they even try it and find they have trouble keeping up with the stairs or getting them to work correctly. What I know is, if they would only ask, someone could show them how to use the computer part in only a couple of minutes. With just a little practice, they could master the stair climbing motion. Perhaps they'll look a little funny learning. But they'll look and feel far better, later on.

Note: Something that can be a lot of fun and that you may well want to consider is mixing aerobic activities like stationary biking and rebounding. You can begin warming up with easy rebounding. After warming up, you could then do some bike riding. You might go back to rebounding for a while and then do more riding. Putting the rebounding between your rides on the stationary bike helps keep your pulse comfortably where it needs to be. You simply alternate going back and forth between the aerobic activities until it's time to finish by gently rebounding to warm down.

Rowing Machines

This exercise device is supposed to give you much the same workout you would get when rowing a boat. It isn't much to look at, but a good rowing machine does a better than good job.

The boat that it simulates isn't a rowboat, but a shell—a fancy, sleek boat that's used in races. Somebody finally realized that the

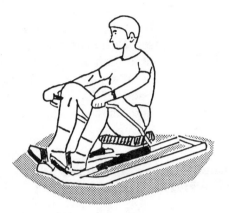

people who rowed shells were typically as sleek and strong as their boats. Because the rowing motion involves so many muscles of the arms, shoulders, back, stomach, and legs, it gives a nearly complete body workout. The machine's seat slides so you can push with your legs as you pull back on the "oars" with your arms. Then, because your feet are strapped down, you pull yourself forward with your feet as you push the oars forward. It sounds complicated but it isn't. Someone with no experience at all would need maybe five minutes to get the hang of it.

A rowing machine provides a good total-body workout. Put it in front of the television or where there's music and add more fun to your exercise sessions.

Here are some features to look for if you decide to buy and use a rowing machine. Be sure the seat is large, well-cushioned, and sturdy, and rolls easily when you're sitting on it. You need to be able to strap your feet into the foot rests comfortably and securely. The oars need to be adjustable to several settings so the effort required to move them can be increased as you grow stronger and increase your endurance.

I bought an apparatus that was advertised as a combination rowing machine and weight lifting device. I paid about $125 for it. The rowing machine part of it has done well, but I haven't found the weight lifting exercises it does to be that helpful. Probably $125 is about the least you'll be able to pay to get a decent rowing machine. What are supposed to be the better ones cost $200 and more. I have one of the "better" ones also and I don't believe it is much better than my less expensive one. The "rowing machine" devices you may see advertised on TV or elsewhere that cost "only $19.95" or some low price like that are likely to be a considerable disappointment.

Is there a particular advantage to the rowing machine over the stair machine and stationary bike?

Probably the biggest advantage is that it gets many more of your muscles involved when you exercise. It works your legs, back, arms, shoulders, hands, and even your stomach muscles. The problem is that it's difficult for most people to stop and take their pulse while rowing. Also, the rowing motion might not get your pulse rate up easily.

Computer-Type Rowing Machine

The graphics (images) you can watch, while you row, makes this machine more motivating and more fun than the regular rowing machine. It makes it more expensive also.

The computer-type rowing machine costs a good deal more than $19.95. I'm convinced it's worth the expense, if you enjoy rowing and can afford it. I use one at the club I belong to. This type of rowing machine has a computer and computer program much like the stationary bike and stair machine I told you about earlier.

A word of caution about rowing machines. If you have lower back problems, take care with the rowing machine. Using too much resistance too soon or using the machine carelessly could hurt your back. When rowing, it's important to keep your upper body fairly erect and lean just slightly back as you pull back on the oars. Each time you pull back, make a practice of tensing your stomach muscles to help protect your back and strengthen your stomach.

The idea in using a rowing machine is to exert only the amount of resistance necessary to keep your pulse rate up and to allow you to move back and forth as if you were actually rowing a boat. Avoid putting on a lot of resistance and struggling with it.

Circuit Weight Training

Doing circuit weight training involves going as readily as you safely can from one weight lifting activity to another. You need to go

quickly to keep your pulse up. Going from one exercise to another too slowly or having to wait reduces the aerobic benefit.

You can use free weights (barbells and dumbbells), but most people seem to prefer the weight machines; they can offer better protection from injury and help you keep better lifting form.

If you decide to use circuit weight training, I urge you to go to a reputable gym where they have full-time, readily available instruction. Find a gym that won't rush you or make you wait more than 30 to 60 seconds between exercises. At first, anyway, concentrate on higher repetitions (15 or more) using superior form and lighter weights. Avoid getting into the trap of simply trying to lift heavier and heavier weights.

Running or Jogging

One reason I didn't list running or jogging sooner was that it can be a difficult exercise for most people to begin with. I recommend starting with walking or rebounding. Later, if you want, begin to run. If you prefer running, you can then do more of it.

You can enjoy running more and avoid injury by using good form. To improve your form while jogging, get a mental picture of excellent form (described later). Then review how each part of your body is moving and get it to fit your mental picture. Repeatedly doing this, especially as a new runner or jogger, will help your form a lot.

Good Running Form

For good running form, do the following:

- Keep your head up and keep your arms and shoulders relaxed.

- Keep your hands at about waist level and gently clasped.

- Make sure you don't raise your knees high. Instead, raise your feet just enough to keep from stumbling, so you are doing much more of a shuffle than a prance. The prancing looks good, but it'll beat the heck out of your knees, hips, and back.

- Land gently on your heels and roll down to the balls of your feet.

How far should I try to run?

Avoid thinking of running in terms of miles. Miles are meaningless. Minutes are what really count. Don't fall into a trap where the goal becomes running more and more miles to try to compete with others. The real competition is with the hurtful stress, and you win against it by running minutes, not miles. I prefer to run a loop—going out and back from a starting point; running around and around on a track can be boring.

Much of the fun of running is to put your body in motion and let it take you for a wonderful ride. You'll fantasize and get into a groove where time passes quickly—often too quickly to suit you. (Writing about it encourages me to go for a run.)

Unless you're actually racing or doing racy thinking, the hardest part of any run is the first part. That's when your body is breaking loose of the "chains" of doing little to free you to play. It will take just a few minutes for you to warm up and for your blood to get moving—then the running gets easier.

I once talked with a woman who told me she had run a mile a day for three years. And she "hated" ("don't like" thinking) every run she did. She said it "always hurt" and "never" ("always never" thinking) got any easier. The fact, unknown to her, was that she had been running the more difficult part of nearly all runs. She didn't run long enough to gain the endurance and strength that would have progressively made the first mile of each run easier. Had she worked up to and run perhaps two or three miles every other day, my guess is she would have grown to love running.

Cold weather running can be a challenge but a great deal of fun. (My all-time best run was during the first part of a snowstorm.) Be sure to keep your head and hands covered and warm, wear layers of athletic clothing, and still drink plenty of water.

The best time to run when the weather is hot is during the cooler parts of the day. Drinking water before and after a run, particularly on hot days, is highly recommended. If possible, you can occasionally stop for a drink during a run.

As with any PlayRobic activity, take your pulse five minutes after your run. If your pulse is still over 100, that's a signal you did more than you needed to do and can ease off, beginning with your next run.

When running on the street, it's important to go against the traffic. It feels strange at first, but it's much safer. You can see what's coming and a driver who is eyeball to eyeball with you is far less likely to see how close he can get to you with his car. Wear a reflective vest, available at most sporting goods stores, when running at dusk or in the dark.

Stretching

While most knowledgeable people who exercise agree that stretching is an important part of physical activity, there's less agreement about when to do it. Some say you need to stretch before you start to warm up. Others say you need to stretch after you've warmed up, but before you begin the main part of your physical activity. Almost everyone agrees it's important to stretch afterward.

I strongly suggest that you avoid stretching until your muscles are warmed up. If you stretch cold muscles, you can easily injure them. Your muscles are something like modeling clay. If you roll it in your hands a little while and warm it, the clay stretches easily. If you try to stretch it cold, it's apt to break.

I like to stretch my larger muscles first, starting with the lower part of my body. I then work my way up to the smaller muscles of my upper body.

It helps to stretch in two phases. (1) Stretch to the point of mild muscle tension, but not strain or pain. Hold it there for a slow count of 8 to 10. (2) Stretch a bit further until you feel the tension in the muscles again. Hold the stretch there for a slow 8-to-10 count. Then go on to the next stretch. Once you've stretched on several occasions, you'll find that you can reliably do it without needing to count.

Getting Ourselves to Play

**I know I need to exercise more, but ("Yes, but" thinking) I
have a hard time getting myself to do it.**

The major obstacle to doing exercise is what we tell ourselves that
keeps us from doing it.

People often tell me that they'd exercise, but they have only so
many hours in the day. It's all they can do to work all day, take care
of their families, and get enough sleep to do it all again the next day.
I tell them that when they are ready to give it a chance, PlayRobics
loves them so much it will give them the time to do it and even
more.

PlayRobics works like this. Part of the reason you need eight or
even nine hours of sleep is because your body tries to make up for its
lack of aerobic activity with sleep. And it is losing ground; it isn't
able to do it.

By doing your PlayRobics, you'll decrease the amount of time
you now need for sleeping. It doesn't happen overnight, but you're
worth the time it takes.

When you wake up after maybe seven hours instead of eight,
you'll feel as though you've been shot out of a gun, all ready and
raring to go.

You can then use part of your newfound time for PlayRobics.
The rest of the time you can take a long hot bath, make love, read, or
do whatever else you enjoy.

Play Aids

If you need encouragement to begin a program of
PlayRobicise (playful exercise), try these aids:

- Occasionally, picture yourself already doing and loving
  your PlayRobics. Imagine it vividly and see it as being as
  positive as you can. You might do some of this daydreaming
  while you're stopped at stoplights or cleaning up around
  the house or yard.

- Pick and use one of the PlayRobics activities you find
  easy, one that you're likely to enjoy. Forget the old notion
  that something has to be hard to do you any good. Pick an
  easy one.

- Involve someone else—a neighbor or family member—in a PlayRobicise such as walking. Take your pulse rates together and compare them at intervals. Tell each other jokes and catch up on the latest news.

- Set specific days and times when you'll treat yourself to the activity you deserve. If need be, tell your family, or whoever needs to know, that those are your times and you expect and have a right to their cooperation. (This may be a good time to practice your constructive confrontation.)

- Use a calendar and put a big check or star on those days you do your loving PlayRobics. You might give yourself a real treat such as a warm bubble bath—almost anything other than hurtful food and drink. It's important to check a calendar or treat yourself immediately after the PlayRobics. Rewarding yourself right away encourages you to keep up your program.

- Mix your PlayRobic activities. One day you might rebound. The next day you might go for a brisk walk, and so on. This kind of variety can be the spice of your happier, excess stress-free life.

- Lively music can be extremely helpful in making your PlayRobicise an even more positive experience. You can use a small radio when you walk or run. Indoors, you might watch television or talk with others.

- Alter your routine. This sounds too simple, but it can be highly effective. Let's say you want to do your PlayRobics as soon as you get home from work, but you almost always find that you get sidetracked. Or, by the time you get home you've somehow lost your enthusiasm. Change the usual routine you follow going home from work. Take a different route. Park your car in a different place or go into your home using a different door. I know it may sound silly, but it works. I've played this "trick" on myself many times.

Scheduling Your Play

When you do your play is an individual matter; you know a lot better than I do what your life is like. Even so, here are some hints you can apply to your own situation.

I'm a morning person. I function better in the mornings than I do at night, so I usually plan to treat myself to my play (exercise) in the early part of the day. I get up before my family and get it done before they start their day. If you function better in the morning, or in the evening, schedule that time to get your playing done.

If you have a lunch hour in the middle of the day or a break in your work hours, and somewhere to clean up after getting sweaty, you may want to exercise at the start of the hour off and then eat a quick meal.

People say, "I just can't ["can't" thinking] exercise when I prefer to, because I need to eat just before. I can't exercise on a full stomach." The growing evidence is that what has been said about not exercising soon after eating may not be true for many of us. We can exercise comfortably soon after eating, particularly when we're doing one of the more highly rated PlayRobic activities such as stationary biking. Test it out and see how it goes. You may find you need to spend more time with the warm-up than you would on an empty stomach. Another aspect working in your favor is that eating and drinking foods that are best for you (low in fat and refined sugar) are easier on your stomach and may well help you to play soon after eating.

It's important—no, it is *crucial*—to avoid scheduling your exercise around everyone else's interests and needs (keeping your light at the feet of others). You deserve special attention too. I know people who think they can only do something for themselves if they are simultaneously doing something for someone else. They will, for example, go for a walk only if their children go along. And their kids couldn't care less whether their pulse rate stays where they need it to be. Some of these people will say, "Well, I'll just have to [duck dialogue] take the children anyway. Maybe the children *will* keep me from going at a pace that will get and keep my pulse up. But something is better than nothing. Right?" Wrong. Please don't kid yourself. Again, you deserve to be taken care of too. Neglect yourself and sooner or later others will suffer for it. You're special and important.

10

Mastering Addictions

Identifying and Dealing with Addictions

When we hear that someone is an "addict," we usually think of drugs such as crack, heroin, alcohol, and maybe nicotine. Many of us wouldn't associate the word "addict" with sugar or chocolate. We'd be even less likely to think of addictions related to hamburgers and other high-fat foods, relationships, sex, extramarital affairs, laxatives, self-induced vomiting, starving oneself, caffeine, soft drinks, money, exercise, work, attention from others, worry, approval, gambling, spending money, television watching, dieting, and even religion.

Many people who are knowledgeable about addictions would agree that some signs of addictions are:

- Addicted persons typically use what they're addicted to in an attempt to feel better or to relieve stress, fear, depression, or pain. Part of the reason they need to feel better is because of the addiction.

- If what's addicted to is stopped, the person addicted is likely to have negative reactions commonly called "withdrawal."

Some substances and actions people are commonly addicted
to are:

cocaine (including crack)	morphine
heroin	alcohol
tobacco (nicotine)	amphetamines
fume sniffing (glue, gasoline)	codeine (other prescription
nicotine gum	drugs)
PCP (angel dust)	caffeine
methamphetamine (ice or	methadone
crystal)	opium

There is far less agreement among the experts about whether
the following are truly addictive. You can decide for yourself.
To help with that, use the inventory you'll find in this chapter.

marijuana	sugar
chocolate	high-fat foods
abusive relationships	sex or pornography
shopping	extramarital affairs
laxatives	throwing up
starving oneself	soft drinks
money	exercise
mescaline	steroids
work	attention from others
LSD (acid)	hashish
worry	approval
gambling	watching television
dieting	religion
housecleaning	risk taking

- Addicted persons experience some immediate "benefit" from
  using what they're addicted to. This benefit may be a high,
  excited state or an unusually calm one.
- In the long term, added stress, unhappiness, ill health, or
  even death results from involvement with the addictive substance or circumstance.

Addiction equals short-term gain for long-term pain.
Addiction is partly encouraged by the deep-down belief that if

something seems to help us to feel good or better it must be okay. What addicts us seems to help at first—but only at first.

- Addicted persons have a longing, desire, or craving for what they're addicted to. That desire typically increases with the passage of time (months or years). Then the desire may level off but it is still damaging.
- Those addicted are unable to maintain moderate involvement with what they are addicted to. Sooner or later, they overindulge.
- Those addicted may show similar physical abnormalities. For example, there may be more or less of a particular chemical in their brain than is usual for most people. *Note:* Some researchers believe these common physical abnormalities are the causes of addiction. However, the use of what's addicted to may result in the shared physical abnormalities.
- There might well be an effort to hide, due to embarrassment or guilt, the amount of involvement, or any involvement at all, with what's addicted to. The classic example of this is the alcoholic who hides alcohol in various places in his or her home or even at work.
- If confronted or criticized about their involvement with what they are addicted to, addicted persons will likely deny responsibility. For example, a heroin addict might blame his or her neighborhood, lack of economic opportunity, and so on.
- Addicted persons make an unsuccessful effort to "cure" or resolve the addiction. This usually takes the form of trying to cut back on the addictive substance or behavior.

Your point, then, is that while we usually think of people getting hooked on things like hard drugs, the fact is we can get addicted to many other things. Also, people who are hooked have some things in common. But what does all this have to do with mastering my stress?

Those who've been experiencing hurtful moods and excess stress are more likely to be addicted. They may have sought to resolve stress or moods by using what they are addicted to. What they've become addicted to now contributes to their stress and moods.

How do I decide if I'm addicted to something?

You can use the following inventory. Write your "yes" or "no" answers to the statements on a separate sheet of paper. You may be answering the statements in regard to a hard drug, or your addiction could be to coffee, gambling, alcohol, or any other addiction listed at the beginning of this chapter.

You'll need some courage to answer the statements as frankly as you can. If you're going to benefit, this is where courage plays an important part.

First, write down in your own terms what substance or action you identify with your possible addiction. If it's smoking, then write "Smoking." You may need more than one word to describe it: "The foods that make me fat." "The way I can't seem to stay away from [someone's name]." Then, read each of the eight statements in the Lovelace Addictions Inventory on page 199, and write down either "yes" if the statement is true of you, or "no" if the statement isn't true of you. Don't leave any blanks.

The more "yes" answers you wrote down, the greater the *likelihood* of addiction. A score of five or more "yes" answers (provided you were honest with yourself) means you're probably addicted in the way I define it. (You have a relationship with something or someone that gives, or used to give, benefits in the short run, but later hurts far more than it helps.) Your addiction is even more likely if statements 4, 6, and 8 were among your five "yes" answers.

If you are upset by what you tell yourself after you take this inventory (as in, "Oh no, this is terrible. I'm an addict."), then use the Three-Part Process in Chapter 7 to straighten out your thoughts. You'll feel much better.

The statements can be answered the way you believe someone else would answer, if that person were being frank. The results can assist you to evaluate whether someone else might be addicted. Use that evaluation for your own good purposes and to assist the other person. Don't say what you believe to be true—that he or she is addicted.

Lovelace Addictions Inventory

Note: Please be frank with yourself when you answer.

1. The substance or action helps to relieve emotional or physical discomfort, or it helps to lift my spirits.

   Yes   No

2. If I stop it, I soon begin to miss it.

   Yes   No

3. I now (or used to) get a high or I get a kick (enjoyment) using or doing it.

   Yes   No

4. Sooner or later, I am hurt because of it or I suffer health problems, financial difficulty, unhappiness, damaged relationships, legal trouble, poor moods or excess stress, or job problems.

   Yes   No

5. I have a definite craving or longing for it.

   Yes   No

6. I'm unable to keep my involvement with it under lasting control. Maybe I do okay for a while, but then it gets to be too much.

   Yes   No

7. At least sometimes, I try to hide my need for it, or feel guilty about it.

   Yes   No

8. I have tried (or thought about trying) to do something, like trying to cut back or even stop, to remedy the situaiton.

   Yes   No

If I gave less than five "yes" answers, does that prove I'm not addicted?

It means either you aren't addicted or you're in the early stages of the addiction. That's the way addictions work. They go in a process that begins with denial or "duck plays ostrich" thinking. Then as the addiction progresses, the person becomes more aware of it and recognizes the need for aid.

The first person to take the Lovelace Addictions Inventory in its final form was a middle-aged woman. She told me that her son and her husband thought she had a "problem with alcohol." She didn't think so. Part of the reason she didn't think so was because she "never" ("always/never" thinking) had hangovers and her drinking didn't affect her work. She had noticed some memory loss, and that bothered her enough to talk with me.

Before she took the inventory, I explained that a score of five or more said to me that she was addicted to alcohol. I also explained the importance of being honest with herself, when she answered "yes" or "no."

As she responded to a couple of the statements, she had obvious difficulty. She would say, "Well that could go either way. It could be 'yes' and it could be 'no.'" Then she would take a deep breath (I guessed that meant she was preparing to face the truth) and would say, "But it's probably more 'yes' than 'no.'"

She answered all eight of the items with "yes."

In anything but a happy tone she said, "Well, I guess that means I am an alcoholic." It wasn't long before she came to the happier conclusion that, "It's better to be an alcoholic and know it than be one and not know it." Then she began, with my help, to work on the problem.

Just because I'm addicted to something, does it mean I need to do something about it?

Not necessarily, since some of the things we're addicted to are less of a threat than others. Statement 4 in the inventory deals with that aspect of addiction: "Sooner or later, I am hurt because of it or I suffer . . . ." The hurt or suffering could take the form of health problems, money troubles, unhappiness, damaged relationships, legal difficulty, poor moods, excess stress, or trouble at work.

Hard drugs like heroin, as well as alcohol, cocaine, nicotine, fatty foods, and sugar are some of the addictive substances that pose the greatest threat to health and life. Caffeine is very hard on our emotions or moods. When combined with cigarette smoking, caffeine becomes even more of a threat because of an increased risk of lung cancer. Sexual addiction, affairs, compulsive spending, gambling, and addiction to work can be very hard on relationships, especially marriages. Drugs such as alcohol also play havoc with family life as well as work and moods.

My point on addictions is: The more significant and hurtful their effect on us, on others, and on our work, the more we need to do something about them. Stress masters seek to rid themselves as soon as possible of addictions that are the greatest threat. Once they are overcome, then other addictions can be eliminated.

You said something before about being addicted to relationships and addicted to approval. Would you explain more about that?

Sure. It happens far too often that we get hooked on other people and call it "friendship" or "love." And often these people care little for us. If they care at all, it's because of what we can do for them. Our involvement with such people may well be a financial and emotional drain with far too little satisfaction or pleasure to justify the cost. We may find ourselves alienated from family or friends because of the addictive relationship. Such a relationship is most likely to be romantic, but can be otherwise.

Addiction to approval or acceptance has many similarities to addiction to relationships except it usually involves "authority figures"—parents, grandparents, ministers, teachers, entertainment personalities, counselors or therapists, and political leaders. A classic example would be a spouse who places more emphasis on the approval of his or her parent than the quality of his or her marriage. Religious followers who give more money than they can reasonably afford are addicted this way. One of the interesting aspects about this addiction is that the one addicted may never have any direct contact with the person to whom he or she is addicted, such as the fan of a movie star. All the "contact" is imagined.

What can I do to get rid of an addiction?

For any addiction, *it's best to assume you are safe only when you are entirely free of it.* For example, most tobacco (nicotine) addicts and alcoholics go through phases where they, at first, tell themselves that the problem is that they just overdo their drug. You often hear statements like, "I know I need to cut back, and I will." Those addicted to alcohol or nicotine ultimately need to come to the conclusion that *any* of their drug is too much.

Once the drug is eliminated, staying free of the drug is taken one small step at a time. Shine your light at your feet as much as possible. You promise yourself to be free of the drug this hour; then this morning; then this day. You take care of the next block of time only when it gets here.

If you "mess up" and use again what you're addicted to, you need to consider that as part of a process of getting free, rather than a failure. You can apply the Stress and Mood Mastery Three-Part Process in writing to the event and learn from it. What were you feeling when you "messed up"? What was the situation? What were you thinking, beneath the surface, that was duck thinking? Counter the duck thinking with eagle thoughts. Doing that is *very* important!

When you do or use again what you're addicted to, *avoid the "big lie"* that says, "*Well, I've done it now, I might as well keep on.*" Doing or using again what you're addicted to is like standing in the middle of a field of very dry grass and, in effect, tossing a lit match into the air. Tell yourself something like, "I tossed a match, but the flame didn't catch, to set my field on fire. I'm not going to toss any more matches. I deserve a lot better than to go up in blazes!" You might get away with tossing one match, or two, or even 200. But if you keep on tossing them, sooner or later you'll go up in smoke—full-tilt back to the addiction.

I can understand what you're talking about where things like alcohol or smoking are concerned. We can live without them. But we need to eat, and if someone is addicted to food, they can't just give up eating.

Foods, exercise, and work we need to do (and can be addicted to) have what I call "critical mass" involved. In atomic physics, radioactive materials are relatively safe—they won't explode, anyway—until you get to a certain amount (critical mass). Then, watch out! You're likely to have an explosion and a deadly mess. You can get away with eating some fattening foods, but once your intake goes over a certain point (critical mass), there's a loss of control. The trick is to keep what you're addicted to safely under that point.

Where food addiction is concerned, the recommendations made in Chapter Eight are geared to helping to keep well under the critical mass amount. By eating and drinking any of the foods identified as "hurtful" or "bad" for us, we're more likely to get into trouble. We're tossing another lit match into the field of very dry grass.

What are some other things I can do to be free of an addiction?

You can use affirmations when you're tempted to be involved with what you're addicted to. You can take out a card with your affirmations on it, read the affirmations, and think about them until the interest in the addiction passes. It's nearly impossible to read positive, life- and love-affirming statements and maintain an interest in doing something hurtful.

Also, the Stress and Mood Mastery Meditation can help. It offers, without doing damage in the process, much of what people get or hope to get from their addictions. These benefits include things like: quick relief from upset, a feeling of well-being, sure escape from worry, greater confidence, calm without a loss of alertness, an ability to think more clearly, and real help to solve problems.

Finally, various self-help groups are available for different addictions. Some of the best known are AA (Alcoholics Anonymous), Gamblers Anonymous, Sexaholics Anonymous, and Overeaters Anonymous (for food addiction). If you need or want to know more about such a group and don't know whom to call, contact your local Health Department or Social Services Department for information. Someone there can tell you what you need to know.

11

How You Know
You're Getting There

*How to Gauge and Ensure
Progress in Mastering Stress*

Remember the stress inventory you took in Chapter 1? Take it again later, after you've had more of a chance to practice BEING—being truthful, aware, self-responsible, living mostly in the here and now, and believing. A lowering of your score can show progress you've made already.

You'll find a copy of the stress inventory you took in Chapter 1 at the end of this chapter.

What if my score is as high as before or even higher? Does that mean I'm going backward?

If that happens, it most likely means one of two things:

1. The first time you took the test, you unknowingly kidded yourself. You scored as low as you did because you weren't

being entirely honest. Now that you're being more truthful, your present score better represents where you actually are. You've made a significant step that you have a right to be proud of.

2. You are not yet applying (or not applying so well) the recommendations made in Chapter 7. And you can change that. You deserve to change it.

If you're not progressing because you're not applying what I've recommended, the reason(s) can be found below:

- You get attention by being stressed or in a bad mood; it's your claim to fame. Believe me, you can get attention in other, better ways and live a far more satisfying life.

- Being in a bad mood or under stress hurts. The hurt you get is the punishment you're subconsciously giving yourself for real or imagined past wrongdoings. Being in a bad mood is also a way of trying to punish others. You negatively influence one or more people around you with your upset. Even if you deserved it at some time past, you've been punished enough. You deserve better now.

- Being stressed and in a hurtful mood is what you are used to. Ever since you were a child, someone (maybe a parent) has been this way. Over the years, you've grown to expect these conditions as a part of living, so you subconsciously make them happen. A rule of human nature is that people will (if they don't look out) hold on to what they're accustomed to, even if what they're accustomed to is hurtful and not worth keeping. Please believe me, you can adjust to being and staying happy and free of excess stress.

- You haven't yet identified the thinking that's really causing your stress or the reason you need your stress—to justify doing an addictive act or using an addictive substance.

I'll illustrate the final reason for not yet progressing, using the case of a woman who smoked and said she wanted my help to stop. She said, "I not only have a stressful job ["makes me feel" thinking] in a nursing home, but I also have three children, five years and younger ["terrible" thinking or "makes me feel"]. I'm divorced. My former husband is disabled and pays no child support, and never ["always/

never" thinking] will. So, I have no ["always/never"] money. I have no ["always/never"] time at all for myself. My car 'died' last week, and I doubt ["I just know"] anything can be done about fixing the engine. I have to ["mind in the gotta" thinking] walk to work and everywhere else I go, or I don't get there."

Her point in telling me all this was to let me know that her stress was beyond any help that I, or anyone else, could offer her. It was hopeless. All of these "tragic" events that were happening to her, that "caused" her considerable stress, could not be changed. No way.

I told her, "You're right. There's little to nothing that can be done about your situation. You need your job and you aren't in a position to change much about it. I'm not willing to take even one of your children, even if you wanted me to. If the court isn't able to, there isn't anything I can do about your child support," and so on.

Then I went on to tell her, very much to her surprise, "The good news is that none of that actually causes the stress that you're having. Those circumstances—your job, children, little money—certainly influence you. But they don't cause your stress. There's a great deal of hope for you, since you don't need to change what isn't changeable to feel much better. What needs to change, you surely can change."

From the look she gave me, I guessed that she thought I was either out of my mind or I didn't yet understand what she was telling me. Had I any idea of what it was like to be in her predicament?

I wasn't at all glad that she was hurting. (She scored very high on the stress inventory in Chapter 1.) Still, I was glad that she was hurting enough to be willing to listen to anything, even my "foolishness," that might possibly help to relieve her.

During my time with her, I shared much of what I've told you in this book. I told her that it was actually what she thought (and rarely knew she was thinking) that caused her stress. She learned that while there was little she could do to change what was going on in her life—how dark her path was right then—she could learn to control how she reacted to it. I shared information about her path and where she needed to shine her flashlight. In other words, I suggested that she pay attention to what was happening in her present reality, rather than worrying about the future or agonizing about her past.

She was surely bright enough to understand and make excellent use of what I shared with her. Still, she didn't seem to grasp it. She said, "What you're saying ["I just know" thinking] is you don't think I have any problems at all ["always/never" thinking]." I told her that I was convinced that she did, and they were serious. They just weren't what she thought they were. She responded with, "You think it's all in my head." I explained that it was in her head in that what caused her stress and sadness was what she was thinking and didn't know about. I wasn't denying that she had strong influences in her life that I certainly wouldn't want them in mine. But she didn't need to wait until they changed to be rid of her stress and sadness. She said, "That's right, I do have bad influences on me. I'd like to see you be calm with all this on you." I still hadn't gotten through to her.

Those who are heavily into duck-like thinking can easily misinterpret some of your reactions to them as a lack of interest and even a lack of caring. They may, for example, be upset and mistakenly attribute their feelings to difficulty at work or elsewhere. When you don't join with them in their upset (and so, imply they're incorrect) they needlessly feel threatened. They may even express this with anger (fear with a mean face) or criticism of you. If you respond with upset (influenced by their anger and criticism), you're saying to them that they are right—you don't think enough of them.

As well as you can, keep your own thinking accurate and respond to those who are upset in a way that's truly in your best interest and therefore is less likely to negatively influence others.

It wasn't until later that I found out the reason I wasn't getting through to her. She was addicted to both nicotine and tranquilizers. And she wasn't yet ready to face her addictions. Without knowing it, she desperately held on to her stress to help explain and justify her addictions: smoking (she inaccurately thought it helped calm her) and taking tranquilizers.

For some, the addiction that inhibits getting rid of the cause of their stress is alcohol. For others, it's smoking. For still others it's being hooked on worry or relationships that aren't working.

If you're having trouble getting what's in this book to work for you, at least consider the prospect that you believe you need your stress and don't know it. You may need your stress to help justify doing something that's addictive. You can use the inventory and other information in Chapter 10 to learn what that addiction might be.

Requiring quick results is a frequent, subconscious strategy to avoid getting what you consciously want. If you have it, fight the demand for rapid relief.

I don't think I'm trying to get attention, or punish anyone, or hold on to what I'm used to. If I am, it's subconscious. But if it is there and holding me back from dealing with my stress, I can see where it could help to know it. How can I find out?

Answer the four statements in the Progress Inhibitor Indicator on this page as being "true" or "false" about you. Notice that each statement has two parts. If either part is true of you, then answer "true."

Progress Inhibitor Indicator

1. I had a serious illness (or was often sick) as a child or teenager, and people were concerned about me.

   Or I was rebellious as a child and often got in trouble because of it.

   True   False

2. A strong sense of right and wrong was a part of my upbringing, so I was encouraged to believe that sooner or later I would pay a price for doing wrong.

   Or I was physically or mentally abused (or neglected) as a child.

   True   False

3. One or more of the grownups who raised me was often upset (perhaps angry, drunk, or mentally disturbed).

   Or My family had a tough time financially and, I believe, was looked down on by people who had more wealth.

   True   False

4. It's likely that I'm dependent on (or addicted to) something or someone damaging to me in the long run (could be smoking, fattening foods, worry, alcohol, etc.).

   Or I don't believe I'm addicted, but one or more other people seem to think I am.

   True   False

Statement 1 has to do with not making progress because you get attention, perhaps mostly negative attention, with your excess stress and moods. Statement 2 has to do with subconsciously using stress and moods to punish yourself and others. Statement 3 deals with holding on to what you are used to. Statement 4 has to do with addiction.

Look at which, if any, of the statements you answered as "true," and you can tell which inhibitor is affecting you. You can tell what, if anything, is holding you back from getting as free of damaging stress as you can and maintaining "eagle moods."

Don't I need to do something else? Is it enough to know there is something in my way and know what it is?

Once you know (and I mean really *face*) what has been holding you back, its power to hinder you begins to wane. The more your conscious mind works on it (as in "Just because I was abused as a child and unknowingly thought of it as punishment doesn't mean I need to keep on punishing or abusing myself."), the more you will be free of it. For subconscious material to continue getting in the way of your progress, it needs to stay in your subconscious. Your conscious mind won't put up with it. Give your conscious mind long enough and frequent opportunities, and it will help you to get and stay free. Once again, *it's so extremely important to substitute eagle dialog and thought for duck.* The more and longer you do that, the better.

The Dying Duck Fit

A woman once told me, "I can't ["can't" thinking] stand it. My husband criticizes me all the time ["always/never" thinking] and so I feel ["makes me feel" thinking] as if I'm worthless [hindsight-labels thinking]. There's no hope ["I just know" thinking] for me as long as I live with him. He's always ["always/never" thinking] going to tell me what to do or lord it over me and yell at me for nothing. I can't ["can't" thinking] stand him. I hate ["don't like" thinking] his guts."

I had already told this bright and capable woman much of what's written here. I told her that her husband could not hurt her with his words. She was hurting herself with what she thought was true. As long as she thought he might be right—that she was a bad person—she would be upset. Once she accepted—I mean *really* accepted—the fact that no matter what he said she was good, then she would not be upset. Once she stopped being upset, he would most likely give up the yelling and criticism of her. But it might get worse before it got better.

Still, the woman wasn't listening. She insisted I tell her what to do to make him be "nice" to her. Or, she wanted me to make him be "nice" to her. Again I told her that the problem wasn't her husband. It was her thinking. She thought things that were entirely untrue. The most hurtful, untrue thing she thought was that she was bad (or not as good as other people) or unimportant or worthless. And much of that was hurt secret self-esteem. When she told herself the truth, she would be happier.

I went on to tell her, "You put yourself at a great disadvantage if you believe that to be in a good mood (happy and free of depression, fear, and excess stress) it's necessary to arrange it so you're only around people who compliment you and are nice to you or that you're in a sunshiny place. Most people and most places just aren't that way! I'm not saying you need to avoid nice places or people who treat you well, but don't depend on them for how you feel."

What I came to understand later was that this woman, while she talked critically of her husband, was (unknown to her) talking about herself. If I had fallen into the trap of talking about him negatively with her, I would have (in her mind, anyway) been confirming that she was "no good."

Still later, I came to understand that she was making a last big stand to hold on to her extreme stress and poor moods. She had been raised in a flock of ducks and was used to the moods and stress. She was used to getting attention by getting upset and she wasn't yet sure she could get enough attention by being happy. What she was having was a "dying duck fit."

Once she was over her "fit," she was then willing and able to consistently apply what she had learned but only sometimes used before.

It sounds to me like she somehow needed to have one last all-out fling in duck-like thinking.

I suspect that's exactly what was going on. In a strange way, her duck fit signaled the beginning of the end of her duck-like thinking and the beginning of far more accurate thoughts. The dying duck inside her was in a kind of death-throe. So, it was an unusual but real sign of progress.

Breaking Out in Smiles

As an indicator that I've advanced in the mastery of my stress, I find myself smiling or even chuckling in response to events I would have been upset about ("makes me feel") before. For example, on a rainy morning I went to a restaurant for breakfast. A large drop of water hit me in the forehead and got my glasses wet. Before, I would have been upset. Instead, I very nearly broke out in laughter. (Each of us has at least some changes that indicate progress to us alone.)

Another example of my before–after change requires a scenario. There we were, Judy, Brian, and I, at 6:20 A.M., still more than a thousand miles from home, and our van was "sick." The motor had raced wildly and the brakes barely stopped us. We ate breakfast while we thought and talked about what to do. Then we checked all the parts that we might be able to fix. Given our limited understanding of auto engineering that took little time. We started off again. Less than three miles farther, we spotted a car dealership. We stopped and were told they could make no promises at all—they worked by appointments. It could be hours or more than a day before they could repair the trouble, and the cost could be considerable. We "camped out" in the reception area of the dealership. After maybe a couple of hours of waiting, Judy said to me, "I'm upset and I don't believe how you're acting. I think the reason I'm upset is the memory I have of how you would have behaved before in such a crisis as this. But here you are calm and cheerful. You don't seem at all worried."

I hadn't realized the difference myself until then. It was true, my level of stress was way down. I was taking this experience as more of an adventure than anything like a crisis. I told Judy, "It proves what's in the book that I'm writing on stress." She said, "I know. And I love it."

Improving Physically

As we begin to master our moods and excess stress, physical concerns (previously brought on by moods and stress) improve. For example, we sleep better, have more energy, grind our teeth less at night, or have fewer stomach aches.

Dr. Lovelace, don't you ever just want to feel bad for a while? I mean, sometimes I want to be mad (angry) for a while. Maybe I could think my way out of it, but I just don't want to. Is that bad, and how do you explain it?

Yes, sometimes I want to be angry or sad or whatever, even though I know my emotion is based on something I believe that's untrue, and I, like you, could talk or think my way out of it. I allow myself to feel hurtful stress sometimes, but less and less often. Holding on to the stress is "bad" in that we are then missing out on a good opportunity to practice stress mastery. But we don't become bad—you and I are still perfect (perfectly us) and that doesn't change whether we practice stress mastery or not.

I suspect this impulse to sometimes be upset is like the urge to scratch a sore that's getting well. The scratching feels good but it keeps the sore from healing as fast as it might. You and I deserve to heal faster.

Finding a Little Tyrant

Here is an advanced stress master's way of checking progress. First, find someone you don't enjoy being around, preferably someone who is critical of you. Then be aware of how you feel being around that person. If he or she is critical of you, are you bothered? If so, you can know you have even more progress you can make. And knowing you can make more progress is an advantage, a positive.

Years ago, I read about people called "los pequeños tiranos" (Spanish for "the little tyrants"). They were identified as being annoying, threatening, and often critical people we don't want to associate with. But they are very helpful to those of us who intend to mature emotionally, stay in control of ourselves and our lives, and be and stay successful. By purposefully associating with "little tyrants" and not letting them "get to" (negatively influence) us, we get the growth we are after.

People sometimes say to me, "My fellow worker [or boss, wife, or whoever] is hard to get along with. He puts me down. He just doesn't seem to like me." I listen to them, but sooner or later I'm likely to tell them that to avoid that person totally they would miss out on a terrific opportunity. That person is their own "little tyrant." That person, if related to well, can be a great help. He or she gives you more of a chance to practice the Stress and Mood Mastery Three-Part Process and to think eagle thoughts.

Duck Dependency

Someone is duck-dependent when he or she relies or depends on someone else thinking duck-like thoughts and staying stressed. In a strange way this dependence is "protective"—or rather, the duck-dependent person believes it is. It "protects" him or her from facing one or more "problems" and from being aware of how badly he feels about himself.

Co-Dependency

What I call "duck dependency" is similar to what others term "co-dependency." My concept of duck dependency is more in line with the original view of co-dependency. Earlier, the label of co-dependency was often reserved for situations involving compulsive behavior or addiction. I don't suggest that limitation for duck-dependency.

Can you give an example?

Sure. The circumstances with a person I'll call Jeff are a good example of duck dependency.

Jeff was often depressed. He was in a relationship with a woman named Toni, whom he cared about deeply. The first time he came for counseling, she came with him. But she refused to return, saying she was made to feel ("makes me feel" thinking) that all Jeff's problems were her fault (a combination of "always/never" and faulty thinking). So, I saw Jeff alone and made recommendations about how to deal with the stress that caused his depression. When his mood began to improve, Toni started to do things such as point out to him tragic events reported in the news. Then one evening, out of nowhere, she expressed doubts about the relationship. She exclaimed, "I don't know if we can make it together." A few minutes later, she told him she was "only kidding" and didn't know what he was so upset about.

At the point Jeff first came for counseling, he didn't yet care enough about himself to justify, to himself, working with me. He was worried about losing [lost thinking] Toni because, being depressed, he was no fun to be around. When she questioned their relationship as his depression lessened, it was all he could do to get himself back to see me.

Why would Toni do that?

As long as Jeff had trouble, she didn't feel so much pressure to deal with her own. His problems kept hers from being recognized. As long as she could influence him to think duck and experience stress, she felt somewhat "protected." She didn't feel so badly about herself—not at the surface, anyway.

Are duck dependents bad people? To me, this woman sounds really mean.

Duck-dependent people are good people. They just don't know it yet. They think they're bad, and so they unwittingly make their behavior match how they feel about themselves. Besides, Toni didn't *make* Jeff have difficulty. He had the depression because of how he thought. But her negative influence *did* make dealing with his sadness more of a challenge. Recognizing that Toni was duck-dependent and a negative influence turned out to be a considerable help to Jeff later.

A woman named Debra came for help to discover what made it so hard for her to "lose weight" and keep it off. Debra wanted to get rid of her fat, but part of her reason for coming was that her husband and grown son criticized her a lot for "being fat." She and I talked about all the diets she had tried. Typically, she would "lose a few pounds." Then she'd weaken and go off her diet. She'd add back the pounds she'd lost and a few more to go with them. As she put it, "The harder I try, the more on my behind I get."

During a lengthy interview with Debra, it came out that her husband was an alcoholic and her son smoked marijuana habitually. Most times when she got on a diet and was doing well, both her husband and son would begin bringing home more of the fattening goodies she had so much trouble staying away from. She then realized that most times she had broken her diet it was with a sugary treat they bought and left out to tempt her.

We speculated that her son and husband criticized her about being fat to encourage the duck-like thinking that led to the stress that led to the anger and fearfulness that she ultimately tried to ease by eating fattening foods. They were duck-dependent on her. As long as she had a problem with food and weight, there was less she could and would say about their problems with alcohol and pot.

Are there any signs that someone is duck-dependent on us?

Yes. Here are some possible indications:

1. As you feel better, as often as not, the duck-dependent person seems to feel worse.
2. Duck-dependent people often talk about negative happenings. They tend to stress the negative.
3. They help you make and maintain excuses for doing hurtful things to yourself. Maybe you stay up too late, and they excuse it by saying it was a special occasion.
4. They're more likely to be critical of you during times when you're down.
5. They seem to do things that influence you so you make yourself angry. Perhaps, for example, they know you hate to be late. Often they're late or they slow you down.
6. Duck dependents regularly give mixed messages that they are unaware of. It can make matters worse to point this out

to them, so it's best not to. They might, for instance, regularly get after you for drinking too much. Then they regularly bring home alcoholic beverages and make it even easier for you to drink.

7. Maybe there's a subject—for example, not enough money to pay bills—that you upset yourself with when it comes up in conversation. The duck-dependent person habitually brings up the subject when you're already tense or sad, even though it's "out of the blue" and has little to do with what has just been talked about.

8. When life is relatively calm, duck dependents are inclined to stir up trouble.

9. A favorite duck-like way of thinking duck dependents have is "poor me" thinking. They "play martyr" in an effort to encourage you to feel guilt. Maybe you haven't mowed the grass or done the laundry. They make a show of doing it themselves, even though it's "your job."

What do you do about people who are duck-dependent on you?

You certainly don't accuse them of being duck-dependent. If they are that way, they're unaware of it. The better way to deal with duck-dependent people is to model (as well as you can) accurate thinking to them. If you don't reward their influence with what they're after, sooner or later they'll tire of their strategy. You can positively influence them as much as they negatively influenced you before. Doing this will make you far stronger in your eagle thinking than you would've been otherwise.

Is there anything else I need to know about duck dependency?

Organizations serve worthwhile purposes. Still, many of them depend on your duck-like thinking to survive. These groups, perhaps more than any other source, encourage you to think inaccurately. So, they definitely support (not cause) your stress.

A few advertisers do their utmost to encourage duck-like thinking and, consequently, stress. They hope that the stress will then lead to an emotion that generates the particular action that the advertiser wants: you buy their client's product or service.

An example would help.

Where I live, a local furniture store regularly advertises the slogan, "Where smart people shop." On the surface, they're saying that intelligent people shop at their store. I suspect that the statement is really intended to encourage the potential customer to do hindsight-label thinking as in, "I'm dumb because I don't shop at this furniture store." Some shoppers act to relieve the stress and hurt self-esteem that result, by buying something there.

Diagrammed, the process looks this way:

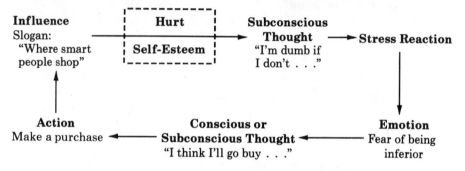

There's an advertisement for a food that uses the slogan, "Real taste, for real people." Isn't that the same kind of thing you're talking about? Some people will interpret the slogan as meaning that there's something wrong with them—they aren't "real people," whatever that means—if they don't eat this food.

Also, other organizations want you to join them or contribute to their cause. A television preacher spent a good deal of time telling audiences, in so many words, "If you don't send money, we won't be able to stay on the air and do good work." Viewers were powerfully influenced to do the mistaken thinking called "terrible" thinking. "Something terrible is going to happen, if I don't send money." Stress was created by this thinking. Anxiety or fearfulness about the continuance of the "ministry" was created by the stress. The fear was relieved by the action of sending money.

Does this mean that groups or organizations are bad?

What I'm getting to is that, to avoid dangerous stress, it helps to have a few guidelines to follow in dealing with groups.

What are these guidelines?

- Be aware of the hidden and implied messages these organizations are putting out. What is the gist of what they're telling you? Is what they're telling you duck thinking? (To suit your own purposes, you may appear to go along with the message, even though you know what they're telling you is false.)
- Deal with groups from your own "*Be* and *Do* and *Have*" perspective. Support them because you are of value, not because you're trying to get to be of value. You already are of the greatest possible importance. No group can change that one way or the other.
- Don't ignore what's truly in your best interest, for the sake of any group. Sacrificing yourself so that others can say, "We must be terrific, for her [or him] to sacrifice herself that way," is far too great a price for you to pay.
- Compare where the organization would encourage you to go with your life (or some part of it) to what your mission is. If the group will, you believe, sufficiently help with (or not interfere with) your mission, then feel free to involve yourself with and support that group.

Okay, I believe I understand. Some groups encourage my stress by urging me to think wrong. They are duck dependents, but they aren't bad, or trying to hurt me. Those organizations are just trying to keep going. I might join or support such groups, depending on whether they help me to accomplish what's important to me. I avoid the stress, in part, by staying aware that the negative messages these groups give aren't actually true.

You've got it.

Criticizing Others

Be aware of how much you criticize others—not because you "shouldn't" (oughty thought) criticize, but because your criticism is an excellent indicator of how you feel about yourself and how well you are dealing with your stress. [This is only a good indicator if you were critical before. Some people dislike themselves and are under considerable stress, but still are rarely critical of others (the passive type of hurt secret self-esteem).]

Since I discovered that when people are critical of others they are (without knowing it) actually talking about themselves, I realized this could be a terrific gauge of my own progress. Not being critical of others means I feel better about myself. Saying kind things about others means I think better of myself.

Using the Three–Part Process

An outstanding way of gauging your progress in dealing with your stress is to notice how much use you're making of the Stress and Mood Mastery Three-Part Process. With few exceptions, the more you use it (at first anyway), the better it is.

Great progress = much use of the process
Good progress = average use of the process
So-so progress = some use of the process
Poor progress = little to no use of the process

The kind of involvement with the Three-Part Process that does the most good is writing down experiences with stress. Keep a small notebook handy. When you recognize stress or the signs, including emotions, that often accompany it, write down what the situation is or what you're feeling.

Follow that with writing what you know or suspect you're thinking that's causing the stress or emotion. Finally, identify one or more of the duck-like ways of thinking you're doing and answer that with the truth.

If I'm not using the process much, what might account for that?

First, you believe you need to wait and use the process on the "big stuff," the times when you're under a great deal of stress or quite upset. The fact is that the process works exceedingly well on the "small stuff." And by using it on the not-so-severe stress and upset, it's even easier to use it later, when it seems to matter even more. I say "seems" because, for most of us, it's the small day-to-day experiences of stress that add up to be serious problems. Don't neglect them or yourself.

The *second factor* that gets in the way of using the process is the belief that you need to be sure of just what you're thinking that's causing the stress. That simply *isn't* a fact. *Guessing is good enough.*

The *third factor* is one I've heard often enough. It goes like this: "I don't know how to answer the duck-like thinking I'm doing. For example, even when I figure I'm doing 'I just know' thinking, it's hard to know what to say to myself that's the truth and will counter it."

What I tell people is that, at first, almost any effort to counter the thinking will do. You might simply say to yourself, "I suspect I'm doing 'I just know' thinking. And it isn't true that I know it." Later, you'll find you can give stronger answers such as, "I'm doing 'I just know' thinking. The truth is that I don't know for sure what's going to happen until it happens. Getting stressed and upset in advance doesn't do me or anyone else any good. In fact, it hurts. I'll shine my light at my feet, where it does the most good. I'll focus my attention on what's happening right now. I can handle that."

This keeping your light at your feet you're talking about still sounds selfish to me. I've got a relative who's always looking out for herself. If we take a trip, for instance, she'll get us a place to stay that's cheap and uncomfortable for me because she's not about to spend an extra penny. She could care less about whether or not I'm comfortable where we stay. And we're sharing expenses. Her light is always at her feet—looking out for herself.

I doubt that the situation with your relative is an example of what I'm talking about. Keeping your light at your feet has much more to do with here-and-now awareness. You need to be aware of and responsive to what's happening in your life, right now. There's also an element of responsibility to it. Keeping your light at your feet means, in part, you're taking responsibility for what you do and have. Shining your light at the feet of others can mean blaming others or circumstances for "difficulty" in your life.

Appropriately shining your light at the feet of others means being responsible *to* others, and usually doing so without the "grate expectation" that they'll do the same with you.

Please Remember

What you learn here can be improperly used as a weapon. This will only happen when you have, as yet, a superficial understanding and acceptance of the truths you find here.

For example, you might say to someone, "You shouldn't be upset at what I did. I don't make you feel anything. If you're upset, it's because you believe something untrue."

While the preceding is based on something that's fact, it is still "oughty" thinking ("You shouldn't be upset . . . .") and talk. Besides, it's your responsibility to be an "accurate influence" on others.

Although we know we're unable to make people feel, we still don't have a license to do anything we want. It's not our place and it's not appropriate to point out to others their duck thinking. It's our place to take care of our own thinking.

Loving Others Is a Good Sign

Stress masters love others as well as themselves. As we increasingly take charge of our moods and degree of stress, our love of others grows. It isn't conditional loving ("I'll love you if you do something I want."). It is increasingly unconditional ("I love you because you're you."). It isn't loving that requires us to be around those we love ("If I'm not with you it hurts so much."). It's love with expectations. We expect those we love to respect our needs and the needs of others, and we confront them when necessary. We repeatedly offer and share our values with them if necessary, yet we respect their right to reject our values.

An Absence of Skill Makes Moods

If I understood you correctly back when we first started, you said that emotions such as depression, anger, and fear aren't necessary. Having one of those emotions says there's an absence of skill. Something isn't known and practiced that could be. All the experts I've read or heard said that at times everyone needs to be and should be depressed or afraid or even angry. It's healthy and natural to be that way sometimes. Isn't that about the opposite of what you're saying?

By now, you know me well enough to understand that I shy away from absolutes such as "always" and "never." I'm not going to say that depression or whatever is "always" unnecessary. The more I know and the more skillful I see others become, the more *I strongly suspect that the presence of such emotions shows a lack of skill.* I now doubt that many (if any) of us ever become skillful enough to be entirely free of such emotions. I disagree with anyone who says that we "should" or it's "right" to experience such emotions. I'm not saying it is wrong or bad to do so; it's probably only unnecessary.

My guess is that many people would be upset after hearing you say that feeling angry, depressed, or frightened says they probably don't have enough skill. They'd feel like you put them down.

What kind of subconscious duck-like thinking do you believe such upset people might be doing?

Probably a combination of "makes me feel" thinking ("He hurt my feelings, when he said I was unskilled.") and "I'm my shirt" thinking ("If I don't have enough skill, that means there's something wrong with me."). If they weren't having those "honest mistake" thoughts, they'd probably be pleased to know that they don't have to settle for less than they are fully capable of.

My first karate instructor was Korean and a master seventh degree black belt. Even though it was nearly 25 years ago, I remember very clearly that one day in class he said in his broken English, "When you get [to] be [a] first degree black belt, you fight, [and] beat up, one maybe two anybody. When you [are] second, [or] maybe third degree black belt, you fight, [and] beat up four, maybe five anybody. But when you [are] fourth degree black belt, you *fight no more.*" That was perhaps my introduction to the reality that with increasing skill there is less and less of the emotions "needed" to hit (anger), or hike (fear), or hide (depression).

The more knowledgeable you are, and the more you apply that knowledge skillfully, the less you think inaccurately at all levels. Because you think more accurately, you experience less dangerous stress and increasingly replace it with love motivation. So there isn't the stress that generates uncomfortable, "negative" emotions.

So I can use experiencing less of these uncomfortable emotions as another signal of my progress. When I do feel angry, sad, afraid, jealous, guilty, and so on, I won't think duck-like thoughts and get after myself about it. Instead, I'll recognize it as a chance to practice what I've learned from you.

There's still another benefit: It rarely happens, but if you find that using what you learn here has too little effect on your stress and emotions, that's a helpful cue to check with your medical doctor. It could be a medical problem (drug or injury) your physician can identify that's causing some of your chronic stress and moods. If so, you can use that help combined with stress mastery for the best possible results.

Aren't there some people who would say that having all these good results and having so little anger, depression, and so on makes people less human somehow? Won't they say that people without these uncomfortable emotions are less interesting and even less effective?

There may be such people. My best guess is that they secretly doubt their own ability to significantly reduce such feelings in themselves, or they doubt their ability to "help" others to do so. They are rationalizing. I have more confidence in them than they have in themselves. Besides, I'm convinced that happiness, love, excitement about living, high self-esteem, trust in one's self and others, and considerable energy are extremely interesting and effective.

Giving Yourself Time and Practice

Remember when you learned to drive a car or ride a bicycle? It took a while (with regular practice and some discouragement) before you began to feel comfortable with it. Weeks, if not months, passed before you felt good at it. Even then, there were times—as with poor weather conditions, darkness, and rough roads—when you seemed just about to go back to "square one" in your learning. You messed up. Did you then say, "Well, I guess I really don't know how to drive [or ride a bike]. I messed up. I'll either need to start again or give it up completely."

Perfect Makes Practice.

You can often get someone to drive for you or double you on a bicycle. Whom will you get to be happy for you? Whom will you get to be free of excess stress for you, increase your chances for a longer life, be successful, love your family and friends for you? You're right, these are rhetorical questions. No one will or can do these extremely important things for you or for me.

My point is: How much more important is mastering your stress and moods than riding a bike or even driving a car? It is far more important. It is of the greatest importance!

Hear, and you will forget.
See, and you will remember.
Practice, and you will BE-lieve!

Our society and other societies put more importance on even riding a bicycle than taking greater charge of our lives. However, you and I don't need to accept it. You and I *won't* accept it!

As with learning to ride a bike or drive a car, stress mastery takes time and practice. To be what you consider good at it may take months or longer. You may at times be uncomfortable—you're not used to the change yet—but the comfort grows. As with learning to drive a car, there are occasions when the "driving conditions" worsen and are a considerable challenge. You may well feel you've gone back to where you started and have learned nothing. Feeling this *doesn't* make it so. You didn't give up on riding a bike or driving a car. *You won't give up on stress mastery either.*

Do you recall me telling you about a brand new Stress Master named Sally?

I think so. Wasn't she the first person you described to me? She was getting along much better with her critical mother, and she was having an easier time at work.

You got it. Nearly a year after I last spoke to Sally, I received a Christmas card from her. The card had the Peanuts character Lucy on the front. Lucy was standing in the snow, wide eyed, with out-stretched arms, and saying, "Did you know that Santa Claus actually keeps three lists? One is for naughty girls and boys, one is for good girls and boys, and a very special list for those like us . . . ."

On the inside of the card there were the words, ". . . who are perfect! Merry Christmas!" (Sally and I know that there is really only one list: people who are perfect.)

A brief note that Sally wrote in the card let me know that her realization of her own perfection was growing. She had gotten an important promotion at work and was still relating better to her mother. She was continuing to review and use the material I wrote for her. Sally said doing that helped her to "further incorporate the principles of Stress Mastery." Then she ended her note to me by writing, "For the first time in many years, I am having a peaceful, relaxed holiday season. Thank you."

Sally isn't a Stress Master because she always ("always/never") uses everything ("always/never") she learned from me or because she's entirely free of harmful stress. She isn't. Sally is a Stress Master because she is willing to change, to accept the truth, to keep on learning and to practice, practice, practice what she has learned. She is willing to do those things because she realizes that she is *worth whatever it takes*. She most definitely is. *You are too!*

Following are additional copies of the Lovelace Stress Inventory you completed in Chapter 1, the Lovelace Secret and Surface Self-Esteem Inventory from Chapter 4, and the Lovelace Addictions Inventory from Chapter 10. If you wrote on them earlier, use these clean copies to complete them again later and compare the results that show your progress.

Finally, there are two pieces of information you haven't seen before that can be very useful. They are the Stress Master's Quick List and the Stress Master's Eagle Aids. Use them often as quick and easy references.

Goodbye, my stress master, eagle-thinking friend. I hope we will talk again.

Lovelace Stress Inventory

Not at All Like Me			**Moderately Like Me**			**Just Like Me**
1	2	3	4	5	6	7

1. I am under too much stress. [Remember, the *more* you believe a statement is *usually true* of you *in recent times,* the *larger* the number you write down elsewhere or circle below.]

   1   2   3   4   5   6   7

2. I worry about people or things.

   1   2   3   4   5   6   7

3. I have a fear that interferes with or holds me back in my life. [This may be a fear of situations such as speaking in public, driving long distances, being in deep water, or riding elevators.]

   1   2   3   4   5   6   7

4. One or more of my relationships at work or at home suffers because of my irritability or anger.

   1   2   3   4   5   6   7

5. I don't believe I'm as successful in my work as I can be.

   1   2   3   4   5   6   7

6. The way I eat and drink is nutritionally very poor, or I eat too much fattening food too often.

   1   2   3   4   5   6   7

7. I have a physical problem that I have been told or I suspect comes from pressures at work or at home. [Examples are: stomach troubles, sleep difficulty, teeth grinding, decreased sexual interest, high blood pressure, excess fat, muscle pains, excessive sweating, bitten fingernails, headaches.]

   1   2   3   4   5   6   7

8. There are too many things I have to do each day.

   1   2   3   4   5   6   7

9. I know or have been told I use too much of one of the following: nicotine from tobacco, caffeine from coffee or tea, alcohol, "nerve pills," marijuana, or hard drugs such as cocaine.

   1   2   3   4   5   6   7

10. I exercise too little or the exercise I do doesn't help that much.

   1   2   3   4   5   6   7

Now, total the numbers you wrote down. You can compare that total with what you got the first time you took the test.

Lovelace Secret and Surface Self-Esteem Inventory

Directions: To select from each of the 20 parts, write down the column letter (A, B, or C) of the statement that *best describes* you. Space requirements have limited the possible descriptions; perhaps only a few of the descriptions will fit you exactly. In some parts, more than one statement might be valid. *Pick the one that comes the closest to describing you.* Avoid responding with what you believe are the "right" answers. *All answers are right when you give the most accurate responses you can.* Write down only one letter in each fill-in space or on a separate sheet of paper, and don't skip any numbered items.

	A	**B**	**C**
____ 1.	When someone says something bad about me, it doesn't really affect me. Or, I like it when someone is bothered by what I do or say.	My feelings are hurt by someone's disapproval of me or of what I do or say.	Someone's criticism of me, if anything, increases my caring about or understanding of the person criticizing me.
____ 2.	I feel I'm able to control what someone does or doesn't do, or control how he or she feels. And I seem to need that.	Too often I feel out of control or powerless. Or I feel manipulated.	I understand that I am in control of myself. No one can control me. And I have little interest in trying to control anyone else.
____ 3.	If anything, I think of myself as being better than other people.	I think of myself as being less important than other people.	I understand and behave like I'm no better or worse than anyone else.
____ 4.	How I look is very important to me. If possible, I want to always look my best and be in fashion.	I don't care that much how I look as long as I'm comfortable and clean.	How I look is important to the degree I want it to reflect how good I feel about myself. (My body is *now* adequately lean and fit and I am usually well groomed and clean.)

	A	**B**	**C**
___ 5.	Actually, I don't mind a good argument. It helps to clear the air or makes life more interesting.	I dislike a fight or argument. And I'll do what I can to avoid it.	I don't try to avoid arguments—they are all right with me. Still, I don't try to win them at other people's expense.
___ 6.	I don't really care about helping other people. I easily turn down nearly all requests for help.	It's about impossible for me to turn down a genuine plea for help.	I help others and I help myself. I won't help others if it means doing harm to myself. I may regularly turn people down.
___ 7.	I believe, or others tell me, I'm a perfectionist. I'm *not* likely to be satisfied until most things are done and done well.	Often I don't care if most things get done or how well they are done. It just isn't that important to me.	I do what I do well because I deserve it. And if I don't do well, I'm rarely bothered at all.
___ 8.	I dislike making mistakes and avoid them whenever possible.	Too often, my life seems to be filled with mistakes. I don't seem to be able to avoid them for long.	I don't usually make mistakes, but when I do I'm not upset much.
___ 9.	If at all possible I don't ask for help. I feel I should be able to do without it.	I ask for help and don't mind it that much. Still, too often it doesn't work that well.	I usually know when I need help, and I ask for it. If the help doesn't fit, I can often get it to work.
___ 10.	I regularly criticize other people and situations. Maybe I shouldn't, but it helps to let it out.	I was taught it wasn't right to criticize, so I avoid it as much as I can. Maybe I do hold it inside.	I'm rarely critical and not because it isn't proper. It's more that my mind doesn't work that way.

	A	**B**	**C**
____ 11.	If someone disagrees with me, I think he or she just has a different opinion. That's okay.	If someone challenges what I believe is true, I more than likely assume I'm wrong. I'll probably change my mind.	If someone challenges what I believe is true, more than likely I think they are wrong. And I want to convince them to think my way.
____ 12.	I'm comfortable with praise, but I don't really need it to feel good about myself and what I do.	I need recognition. Most everyone needs praise for the good they do or for what they accomplish.	I don't much care if I get praised or not. In fact, I tend to feel uncomfortable being fussed over.
____ 13.	It just doesn't normally occur to me to pay attention to who likes me and doesn't or how many friends I have.	Not many people like me. Or the ones who do like me I don't care for that much.	I have (or hope I have) many friends and keeping those relationships is very important.
____ 14.	Material goods or success comes to me as a kind of byproduct of living my life happily.	I don't much care about getting ahead. It's just more to keep up with and be concerned about.	Getting ahead in life—career success or having valuable things (or success as a homemaker)—is important to me. And I'm working hard for it.
____ 15.	I'm normally too busy enjoying or learning from what's going on now to think or talk about past accomplishments.	There isn't that much I have to be proud of. Or there is and I keep it to myself because it isn't right to brag.	At times anyway, I'm quick to let others know about what I've accomplished or the good things that happen to me. I'm not real shy about singing my own praises.

A	**B**	**C**
___ 16. I'm entirely responsible for what happens in my life. Blaming others or circumstances doesn't make any more sense than feeling badly about the past you aren't able to change.	Many of the bad things that happen to me are my fault. I feel guilty about or regret such mistakes.	If things go wrong, it usually isn't my fault. Other people or circumstances are probably to blame.
___ 17. There is a sense of positive direction to my life that somehow comes more out of my great worth as a person than out of goals I set and reach.	There seems to be little to no direction to my life. It's hard to imagine things getting to be good for me.	I often do (or think I should) set goals or objectives and evaluate my progress in attaining them. If life gets tough, I can think about how good it can be some day.
___ 18. My usual manner could best be described as "happy." When needed, I easily speak up for myself without being harsh. I do confront well.	I'm usually reserved. I don't speak harshly to others and try always to be considerate, even if it means my needs go unmet. I don't confront all that well.	I have something of a blunt or brusque manner. I'm rather outspoken and it sometimes comes across to others as "mean" or "aggressive."
___ 19. Whether "fair" or not, people do what they believe is in their best interest. I don't think that's wrong. It's just how people are.	Most people look out for themselves and will pretty much do whatever they think they can get away with. It's not right, but it's how people are.	I have definite beliefs about what is and is not fair. And I'm upset when I or others are treated unfairly.
___ 20. I know that what others say will not hurt me. It's only what I say that hurts me.	I am careful about what I say, because I might hurt someone else.	I am careful about what I say, because someone might use it to hurt me.

____ 21. Write down the number below that best describes how you *now* feel about yourself. The 1 at one extreme stands for absolutely hating yourself. The 7 at the other extreme stands for the very best you can possibly feel about yourself. Perhaps a number in between the two extremes better describes how you now feel about yourself. Please write or circle a number now.

Totally Hate Myself						**Totally Love Myself**
1	2	3	4	5	6	7

Lovelace Addictions Inventory

Note: Please be frank with yourself when you answer.

1. The substance or action helps to relieve emotional or physical discomfort, or it helps to lift my spirits.

   Yes   No

2. If I stop it, I soon begin to miss it.

   Yes   No

3. I now (or used to) get a high or I get a kick (enjoyment) using or doing it.

   Yes   No

4. Sooner or later, I am hurt because of it or I suffer health problems, financial difficulty, unhappiness, damaged relationships, legal trouble, poor moods or excess stress, or job problems.

   Yes   No

5. I have a definite craving or longing for it.

   Yes   No

6. I'm unable to keep my involvement with it under lasting control. Maybe I do okay for a while, but then it gets to be too much.

   Yes   No

7. At least sometimes, I try to hide my need for it, or I feel guilty about it.

   Yes   No

8. I have tried (or thought about trying) to do something, like trying to cut back or even stop, to remedy the situaiton.

   Yes   No

Stress Master's Quick List

- *"Makes me feel" thinking.* You have an entirely untrue belief (honest mistake) that other people and circumstances create your stress and uncomfortable emotions. What you *think* (and don't realize) really decides your level of stress and your moods. Change that unknown thinking and how you feel about yourself. You are worth the work.

- *"I'm my shirt" thinking.* You've got the notion that your essence and your value are somehow determined by what you do, think, have, or feel. Wrong! The truth is that what you do, think, have, or feel is no more you than your clothing is you. You are of the utmost value, no matter what!

- *"I just know" thinking.* You are not a fortune teller or mind reader. If you worry and are wrong (you worried needlessly), you hurt once. If you worry and are right (the worst *did* happen), you hurt twice. Once is more than enough and is usually unnecessary.

- *"Makes me do" thinking.* This is the untrue thought that you do what you do because you have to; that other people, commitments, or situations force you to act in particular ways. Not likely! You don't "have to," when there are options—even "bad" ones. Take responsibility and take control.

- *"Terrible" thinking.* You don't know something is "terrible," "bad," "the worst," "just awful," "horrible," or "tragic" until you know

233

how it has turned out. It may eventually be terrific. Use such labels sparingly and only when you can reasonably judge.

■ *"What people say" thinking.* What people say isn't nearly as important as what they mean. People too rarely say what they mean, particularly if they are upset or are duck-like thinkers anyway. (It isn't true that people are more likely to tell the truth when they're upset. They are only more apt to blurt out what they think is true and probably isn't.)

■ *"It's not fair" thinking.* From your childhood and from playing games with rules, you've kept the false belief that life, other people (including spouses), nature, or whatever happens should treat you fairly. But life isn't a game. Life is life—not fair. Fair is where you find ferris wheels. You can count on being treated in ways that others believe (consciously or subconsciously) to be in *their* best interest. You fully deserve to do the same. When you are doing what's truly in your best interest, you are increasingly free of damaging stress and uncomfortable moods. You are more unconditionally loving of yourself and others.

■ *"Racy" thinking.* This thinking leads to being in a hurry, and most hurrying is needless. Life isn't a race track where you pause only briefly to make "pit stops." What you're rushing for is rarely, if ever, worth the price you pay. "Racy" thinking often takes over when you're in automobiles or when you're getting ready to go somewhere.

Stress Master's
Eagle Aids

■ *Stress and Mood Mastery Three-Part Process.* First, write down the situation you are in and your emotion. For instance, "I'm getting ready for work, and I feel tense." Next, write what you might be thinking but aren't consciously aware of. (Guess, if you don't know.) "I'm probably thinking: I'm going to get to work and there will be a problem waiting for me." Finally, write down what kind of duck-like thinking you're doing and write out a counter to it. "I'm doing 'I just know' thinking. I am not a fortune teller, so I have no license or right to be telling my fortune. I need to shine my light at my feet and take care of what's actually on my path now, rather than dwelling on future events that may or may not happen." (Note: While it is important to write out the three parts whenever possible, don't *not* do the process because you aren't able to write it down. Perhaps you are driving, for example. You don't write the process but you need to think it through.)

■ *Affirmations.* Write down and regularly review short, highly positive statements to help heal your secret self-esteem and avoid stress. Some samples are:

"Yes! I'm worth what it takes."

"With each passing day, I care more for myself and others."

"I am a stress master and eagle thinker."

"With each mistake, I learn more, and knowing more adds to my great value."

■ *Stopping duck thoughts.* If you find yourself dwelling on some negative thought, or worrying, write some affirmations on a card and keep it handy. You might also write out the appropriate counter to the thought you're stuck on. This is your "I choose truth" list. The true statements, when repeatedly read, will serve to cancel out the stubborn duck thought.

■ *Recognize and eliminate duck dialogue.* When you catch yourself using mallard mumblings such as "can't," "have to," "makes me feel," "just know," "never," "shouldn't," let that be a signal to you: your subconscious stream of thought is filled with untrue and harmful thoughts that create stress. Set about getting those words out of your conscious talk, to help clean up your subconscious stream of thought.

■ *Use your imagination.* Your ability to imagine, which can be your most powerful tool for stress mastery, is often the negative influence (you may or may not realize it) that encourages your duck-like thinking. Turn it around and use this powerful force, so readily available to you, to avoid stress. You might:

—Imagine two unconditional love letters to yourself, one written by you and the other by someone who didn't give you the love you deserved before. Then put the love letters into a very special liquefier. Next, think of yourself drinking the liquid and feeling its sweet nourishment going to every cell of your body. Feel it being pumped, in surges, from your heart and rushing through your blood vessels. Clearly imagine that tiny copies of the original love letters go to every cell in your body. Each cell accepts and benefits from those notes to you.

—Use vividly imagined volume knobs to decrease duck-like thinking and increase eagle-like thinking.

—Regularly think of yourself walking along a forest path and shining your flashlight at your feet. See yourself easily stepping over and around obstacles in the path. Picture the words "calm" and "love" on signs alongside the path.

■ *Stress and Mood Mastery Meditation.* On most days, to maintain your stress mastery, practice this wonderfully calming meditative procedure as described in Chapter Seven. *Note:* An easy way to do this is to get a cassette tape I recorded for you. You'll find information about how to order the tape in the back of this book.

■ *Just say "quack."* When you find yourself feeling stressed or upset, forcefully say the word "quack." You can yell it out in your imagination or actually shout it while alone in your car or elsewhere. Repeat, as needed. "Quack" is a quick way to distract yourself from the untrue thoughts that cause your stress.

■ *See with eagle eyes.* Think of yourself as having wonderful eagle eyes that allow you to observe others (no matter how "nasty" or critical they are) and your surroundings without generating stress. *Don't forget to see yourself with your eagle eyes.* Practice while looking in a mirror.

■ *Make an eagle's mission.* Particularly if you sometimes feel "lost" or uncertain about where you're going with your life, create and write down a mission for yourself. (See Chapter Seven for help with this.) Rewrite it, if need be, and review and think about your mission on a regular basis, maybe each night before you go to sleep or each morning as you begin your day.

Index